Bulldozing The Way
From
New Guinea To Japan

Bulldozing The Way From New Guinea To Japan

Peter D. Davidson

2009

ISBN: 978-0-557-11199-2

Library of Congress Cataloging-in-Publication Data

Davidson, Peter
        Bulldozing The Way From New Guinea To
Japan

145 Pages.

To the GIs Who Did Not Make It

Contents

Description	Source	Page
Theater at Tanauan	Battalion picture	72
Third Platoon, 1897th Headquarters Company	Battalion picture	72
Map 4- Tanauan to Puerto Princessa, Palawan	Unknown	73
A Japanese Zero on the Edge of the Puerto Princessa Air Strip	Personal photo	74
A Caterpillar D-8, the Largest Bulldozer at That Time	Personal photo	84
Palawan Airstrip	Army Air Corps	85
Grading for a Hospital	Personal photo	86
Field Hospital Puerto Princessa	Army Air Corps	87
Barber Greene Model 44C Ditching Machine	Personal photo	88
Landing by LST on Okinawa	Battalion picture	91
Okinawan Thatched House	Personal photo	93
Motobu Peninsula – Airstrip in Background, Ie Shima in Distance	Battalion picture	95

This book describes the everyday life and problems of the enlisted men in the 1897th Aviation Engineering Battalion from stateside training to New Guinea, the Philippines, Okinawa and Japan from February 1943 to January 1946. The 1897th was not a combat outfit but did suffer a number of non-fatal casualties from enemy action.

The problems of ordinary military life in the South Pacific were greatly different from the well-documented campaigns in Europe and North Africa. Americans are familiar with the U.S. Marine Corps land battle at Guadalcanal, but other battle areas of the South Pacific are less well understood though their casualties were higher and their strategic importance was great.

The primary purpose of the 1897th and other Aviation Engineering battalions was to build airfields essential for MacArthur's advances from New Guinea to Japan. Each airfield would have been a major project in any area of the world. These facilities were constructed in tropical jungles with trees up to eight feet in diameter, in swamps where it rained every day, on small islands where coral for airstrips was scraped from the sea at low tide, and in remote areas where supply delivery was uncertain and subject to enemy attack. In addition to airfields, the 1897th built hospitals, roads, warehouses, recreational facilities and any small projects the brass fancied.

This is the story of how the men of the 1897th performed these projects while coping with the tropical jungle, rainfall, malaria and assorted tropical diseases, serious and sometimes fatal accidents, high humidity and temperatures, long working hours, limited recreation and no beer. Each major project took about three months to complete although in some cases an airstrip was in use ten days after construction had started.

Whenever we received a beer ration and an announcement was made that there was to be professional entertainment from movie stars from the States we knew we were headed for another invasion.

CHAPTER 1
Stateside

My three-year Army career commenced with being drafted in Oakland, California, on February 5, 1943 right after my twentieth birthday. I was in my third year in the College of Chemistry at the University of California, Berkeley. From Oakland I was sent to Monterey, California, where the Army spent a month making up its mind where I was needed the most. From Monterey I was sent to Keesler Field, Mississippi, for Air Corps basic training.

At Keesler Field our first rifles were wooden but we were eventually issued British Enfields. The big event each week was the Saturday inspection on the concrete taxi strip in the Mississippi sun. When someone fainted, the man behind caught him and dragged him to the side. The battalions were rated on the number of men fainting at Saturday inspection.

Upon completion of basic training a large group of us was sent to Fort Belvoir, Virginia for construction engineering training. On the train I came down with measles but was still compelled to stand inspection and leave the train to eat when we stopped. I remember climbing stairs to a cafeteria to eat and wondering if I would make it but I did not collapse. On arrival at Fort Belvoir the powers-that-be decided I should no longer contaminate the rest of the Army and I was given my own private rail car on Fort Belvoir's own railroad to ride into camp. After a week in the hospital I was declared fit to continue my engineering training.

I was assigned to concrete paving school but this included other equipment, operation of diesel engines and construction equipment in general. Upon completion of the Fort Belvoir training I was sent to Richmond Army Airbase for my permanent assignment.

The 1897th Engineering Aviation Battalion was just being organized at RAAB. The purpose of the battalion was to build airstrips for the Air Corps. There were four companies, Headquarters, A, B, and C for a total of over 800 men. I was assigned to Headquarters Company as a heavy equipment operator. Our training included the building of bridges, camouflage, booby traps, demolition, infantry tactics and marksmanship. I qualified as an expert with the M-1 Garand rifle.

Our company personnel included a West Point captain, junior officers who had graduated from officers training at Fort Belvoir, a colonel and staff officers who had been professional engineers in civilian life, and senior non-coms who were experienced construction workers, surveyors, machinists, diesel mechanics and draftsmen.

The 1897th was organized by November 1943 and we moved into the woods in tents to practice building an airstrip. The training was not productive because of a lack of equipment, the snow and the mud. I drove a four-wheel drive, ton and a half dump truck to supply coal to the tents. The mud was often so deep I would have to run out the cable winch on the front and winch myself from tree to tree. I ate Christmas dinner standing up in a tent. Before I emptied my aluminum mess kit, the turkey gravy froze to the sides.

In January we continued our training for the South Pacific. We were roused at four AM, loaded into trucks and driven to Virginia Beach to commence our beach landing and crawling-under-enemy-fire training. We were led to a muddy field covered with double apron barbed wire and razor wire fencing. We were to crawl under this carrying our M-1s with live machine gun fire inches overhead. Unfortunately the lieutenant in charge discovered that the mud was frozen solid and this would not do. He had the fire hoses brought out and we wet down the field until it was an acceptable grade of muddiness. Then we crawled under the barbed wire and live machine gun fire. We did keep our heads down. When we exited the other side we lined up for rifle inspection. If your rifle was inoperable you crawled through the mud again under the wire and machine gun fire.

The next exercise was to practice beach landing from landing craft in the surf. We were soaked up to our armpits and Virginia Beach in January is not like the South Pacific. Fortunately we were given a warm place to dry out and don dry clothes.

The end of February 1944 we took a train for California to ship to the South Pacific. The train took us to an Army base at Pittsburg, California, and on March 9, 1944, we boarded a ferry to Oakland, California. At a pier in Oakland with rifle, backpack and duffle bag we climbed aboard a Victory ship to New Guinea with a band playing.

I was assigned to kitchen police serving sauerkraut and wieners as we went out the Golden Gate. I will long remember the chow line faces turning green when we encountered the long Pacific swells going out the Gate as they looked at the wieners and sauerkraut swooshing back and forth. Many then dumped their mess kits in the garbage and ran for the nearest head.

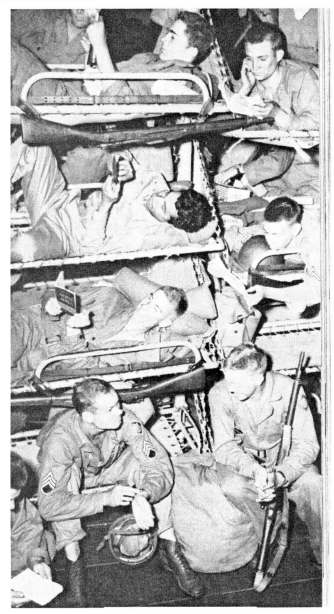

Troop Ship

A Victory ship is about 12,000 tons displacement with a maximum speed of 13 knots. We sailed all the way to New Guinea with no escort for submarines but we did take a circuitous route south of the equator, near New Caledonia and then north to New Guinea.

The picture, "Troop Ship" on page five shows what it was like, thirty-two days from Oakland to Finschhafen. Bunks were stacked 15 high in the bow. Exercise was thirty minutes a day on the deck. We lined up twice a day to fill our canteens with the only fresh water available. This was barely enough for drinking. For shaving and bathing there was cold salt water. When there was a tropical shower, everyone would go out on deck for a fresh water bath.

We lined up twice a day for chow. The two meals per day were served continuously for twelve hours. You ate standing up in the dining area. There was not enough room for chairs. Kitchen police in the tropics was not easy. Kitchen galley temperatures reached 140 °F. You worked thirty minutes on and thirty minutes off, unless you collapsed.

The big recreation besides reading was gambling. Initially it was poker but when most of the money had been accumulated by a few winners, the crap games started. The crap games went on twenty four hours a day until all the gambling money was in the hands of a few successful players. Thousands of dollars were sent home by each of the big winners.

Crossing the equator was occasion for a big celebration. The junior officers suffered most of the initiation rites. Our platoon lieutenant, Gruska, had half his black mustache shaved off. We all received certificates making us "Shellbacks", the honorary title for someone who has crossed the equator.

Thirty one days from Oakland we arrived at Milne Bay, New Guinea.

CHAPTER 2
South Pacific

Before going further it is necessary to explain why we were in the South Pacific and what an Engineering Aviation Battalion was.

Map 1 (pg.10)- South Pacific, includes the Pacific area in which the 1897th Engineers were active, the Southwest Pacific Area where MacArthur was Commander-in-Chief and the Pacific Ocean Area where Nimitz was Commander-in-Chief. In general, the SeaBees built the air strips in Nimitz's area and the Aviation Engineering Battalions built the air strips in MacArthur's area.

MacArthur's overall strategy was inspired by the Buna/Gona campaigns which resulted in more casualties than Guadalcanal. The Japanese were dug in at the Buna and Gona coastal settlements and supplied from Rabaul. MacArthur finally sent General Eichelberger to take charge with instructions not to return alive if the Aussie/American forces were not soon occupying Buna and Gona.

Map 1 - South Pacific Area

The high casualties were little publicized in the United States because most of the casualties were Australian. MacArthur resolved in the future to avoid both high casualties and long delays by hitting the Japanese where they were not and where they least expected it. His first strike of the new strategy was Los Negros in the Admiralty Islands. Although against the advice of his staff and the Navy, this was an outstanding success. Los Negros yielded an airstrip that helped neutralize the big Japanese base at Rabaul and provided air cover for the next strike at Hollandia. Before the Japanese airstrip on Los Negros could be used routinely by American planes, aviation engineers rebuilt the strip to conform to American standards.

The strategy of by-passing Japanese strong points, defined by MacArthur as leap-frogging, required air cover to neutralize the strong points. The effective bomber range was perhaps 1000 miles but for fighter planes it was preferably less than 250 miles. This meant building airfields within effective range for protection of the next planned strike. Each new invasion thus required one or more engineering battalions landing at D-day to commence building the airstrip or strips for the next invasion.

Emblem of the 1897th Aviation Engineering Battalion

The primary purpose of an Aviation Engineering Battalion was to build airfields. The secondary purpose was to construct any facilities required by the Air Force or the Army. The 1897th was normally attached to a large organization such as an Air Force or an Army.

The largest engineering organization is usually the battalion. The battalion is commanded by a lieutenant colonel with a major as executive officer. Each of the four companies; Headquarters, A, B and C; had a captain and four lieutenants. The Headquarters (HQ) company included an administration group with a warrant officer and a master sergeant, a medical group with a doctor and dentist and an engineering planning group with civil engineers (one lieutenant and one tech sergeant), surveyors and draftsmen.

The HQ company contained most of the experienced heavy equipment operators, mechanics, electricians and the machine shop.

For weapons each company had a 37 mm anti-tank gun (later replaced with bazookas), 50 caliber water cooled anti-aircraft machine guns, and a half-track with 30 caliber machine guns. The enlisted men were armed with Garand M-1s and the officers and top non-coms with 45 caliber automatics or 30 caliber M-1 carbines. There were some 45 caliber grease guns available.

Most of the heavy construction equipment was assigned to the HQ company. Caterpillar D-8 and D-7 tractors were the most used earthmoving equipment. All of the tractors except one hydraulic D-8 were cable operated and could be connected to a blade or a carryall as required (12 cubic yards for the D-8 carryall and 10 cubic yards for D-7s). HQ company had two LeTourneau Turnapulls (15 cubic yards) for long distance dirt moving. Other major dirt movers were dump trucks (five ton) and two power shovels (two cubic yards).

For finishing, grading and material handling there were Caterpillar motor graders, one ditching machine, a tow grader, sheep's foot rollers, pavement rollers (water filled), a truck crane and a Turnacrane. Paving was often with steel landing mat initially. Depending on materials available and the weather the preferred final surface for landing strips and taxi ways was compacted coral sealed with asphalt. The battalion had an asphalt plant consisting of two tank trailers with heating coils, a 125-psig steam boiler and a heated tank truck asphalt distributor. The asphalt was melted and cutback with diesel for paving or cutback to a lower viscosity for spraying as a seal coat.

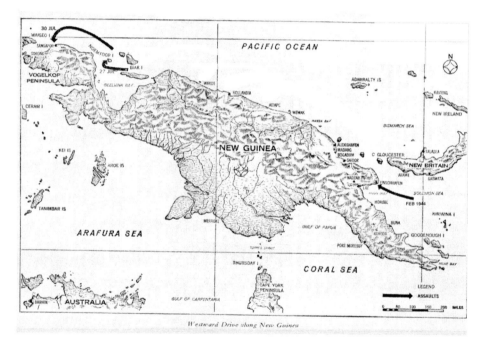

Map 2 – New Guinea

New Guinea's first recorded sighting by Europeans was in 1512 by two Portuguese explorers. Dutch explorers followed and named it New Guinea because of similarities to Africa. Until World War I the island was partitioned between the Netherlands, Great Britain and

Germany. After WW-I the German territory, northeastern New Guinea, was ceded to Australia and the entire eastern half of New Guinea became Papua. The Dutch part of New Guinea, the western half, is now part of Indonesia and is the province of West Irian.

New Guinea is the second largest island in the world, 1500 miles from the eastern tip, Milne Bay, to the western tip, the Vogelkop Peninsula. The northern point of the Vogelkop Peninsula, Cape Sansapor, is only 30 miles south of the equator. A mountain range runs down the center of New Guinea that is high enough in the western half (Indonesian half) for snow. In West Irian the mountains are known as the Schneegebergte and in the eastern half (Papua) as the Owen Stanley Mountains. These mountains are steep, covered with rain forests and cut with deep ravines and rushing streams. The northern half of the island, which is mountainous to the sea, has most of the settlements and a limited development of coconut plantations, oil wells and mining. The southern half of the island is swamp except for the eastern portion that includes Port Moresby. There are few towns in the southern swampy part of New Guinea and the inhabitants are mostly aborigines.

The lower elevations of New Guinea are heavily forested with a tropical climate, a wet season and a dry season. The jungle is thick and you quickly become exhausted hacking out a trail with a machete. Vines ten inches thick tie the trees together near the tops. There are some banana and papaya trees but a non-native cannot live off the jungle without special training.

Mosquito borne diseases such as malaria and dengue fever are endemic. Mite typhus and diseases from fungus such as jungle rot are common. Even the clear, cold streams from the mountains carry cholera, amoebic dysentery and other intestinal diseases.

The American armed forces under General MacArthur established strict rules that minimized the chances of contracting these tropical diseases.

- Sleep only under a mosquito bar.
- Do not sleep on the ground but in a cot isolated with legs in cans of diesel or in a jungle hammock.
- Spray your tent and mosquito bar with an insecticide twice a day.
- Drink only filtered, chlorinated water.
- Wash clothes often and treat the outer garments with insect repellent.
- Wear clothes buttoned at the neck, ankles and wrists.
- Wear boots with leggings.

Conforming to these rules in combat often was not possible and the restrictive clothing was uncomfortable in the tropics.

CHAPTER 3
Finschhafen

A one-day sail from Milne Bay brought us to Finschhafen, New Guinea. The Australians took Finschhafen from the Japanese in October 1943 so by the time we arrived in April of 1944 the only military activity was a few air raid alarms. There were wrecked Japanese landing barges on the shore, courtesy of the Australians, from the Japanese attempt to retake Finschhafen.

On arrival at Finschhafen after over a month aboard ship we were in poor shape to carry our gear in the heat up the hill to the waiting trucks. A few fainted from the exertion. The trucks dumped us into the middle of the jungle where we were supposed to clear camp with bayonets and a few machetes. Fortunately our officers were able to borrow a bulldozer and camp construction started.

We were guests of the Aussies. We used Australian money and were welcome at the Aussie PX with its large tea urn of hot, black, sweet tea available twenty four hours a day. The Aussies were quite a contrast to the Americans. We soon were living in a tent city back in the jungle with company streets and drainage ditches laid according to regulations. We slept on cots with mosquito bars and the inside of each tent was sprayed twice a day for insects. The legs of each folding canvas cot were placed in a can full of diesel to keep various crawling creatures from sharing your cot. The Aussies lived under trees next to shore where there was a cool breeze. They used any kind of tent or piece of canvas with no pretence of company streets. They hung hammocks wherever convenient with or without mosquito netting. They dressed in shorts or whatever was comfortable. We drank chlorinated water; the Aussies drank beer.

We landed in New Guinea during the dry season. During the dry season it rained once a day and during the wet season it stopped raining once a day. Fortunately we completed our jungle camp before the rainy season started. The humidity was always high and any leather quickly turned green with mold. At the beginning of the rainy season the inside of our five man tent was dry. When the rain started the inside of the tent was dry but water gradually soaked in from the outside and the dry circle of earth around the tent pole became smaller every day until one day it disappeared. Naturally all of us wanted a board, a piece of sheet metal or something dry to place our feet on when we swung out of our cot in the morning. Stealing a board or something to stand on was a major crime and nothing was

18

permitted unless the material was issued for the entire company.

Other creatures were looking for a dry place during the wet season. One morning I was trying to pull on a boot but something was jammed in the toe. Suddenly this something wiggled. I became wide awake and grabbed my bayonet. I pried out a land crab that was obviously too large to fit into my shoe.

On another occasion I woke up in the morning feeling a wriggling on my chest. I swung over the edge of my cot and discovered a scorpion building a nest in the hair on my chest. I flicked him off on to the ground where he sat with his poisonous tail flicking back and forth over his head.

Australian Army rations were our meals at Finschhafen. Bully beef, dehydrated potatoes, dehydrated eggs, dehydrated carrots and canned beet tops. Who ever heard of canning beet tops? Bully beef three times a day. However, the New Zealand jam was good and U.S Army bread was always good. The Finschhafen camp was to acclimate us to the tropics while waiting for our construction equipment to arrive. We were kept busy building roads with borrowed equipment, constructing warehouses, drainage ditches and supporting facilities. We had little interaction with the natives although we did visit a few villages as shown in the following picture.

Visiting New Guinea villages in Papua was not popular because of the local custom of retaining the dead, unenclosed, in their former homes. The stench was unbelievable.

The following is a typed copy of the first of my overseas letters that survived. This July 2, 1944 letter is to my mother's first cousin, Warren Manter, a retired master sergeant who had served in the so-called Philippine Insurrection when MacArthur was there as a second lieutenant. Naturally Warren understood my situation and the Army lingo better than most of my correspondents.

Until the war was over all of my letters were censored. Specifically I was not permitted to say where we were, what we were doing or why we were doing it. Sometimes we were not permitted to give the date or describe the countryside. Without background, reading the letters and looking at the pictures will not make sense to anyone who was not there.

New Guinea
July 2, 1944
Dear Warren,

At last it looks like I am going to have a tent with a floor. I'll probably move before, however. I'll miss the familiar squish-squish when I roll out of my cot.

In the column you sent on New Guinea I noticed that a place with which I am very familiar was underlined in red.

I have been running a ditch digger at the hospital where there are a lot of New Britain casualties. After seeing some of the arm-less, leg-less and faceless inmates I am glad I am not in the infantry. There were a couple of tall Sikhs there with red turbans who were amazed by the ditch digger. They had been released by the Japs on Los Negros.

For lack of anything better I shall relate a couple of stories about Jap fighting ability that an Aussie told me. He said that during the battle of Sattelberg they had a Jap detachment cornered in a large patch of kunai grass. It would have been suicide to go in after them but while they were trying to decide what to do the Jap bugler came out and blew "charge". The Japs came out and were mowed down by machine gun cross fire. The Aussie captain bellowed to his men that he would shoot the first man who shot the bugler. The bugler repeated his performance twice again - Japs wiped out, Aussies - one man wounded.

Another time the Japs pulled a sneak raid on a beach in landing barges. The landing would have been a complete surprise if the bugler hadn't sounded, "charge" waking up every

Aussie in the neighborhood. Forty Japs were killed on the beach without an Aussie casualty. There is a sign there to verify this not to mention the remains of landing barges.

Peter

By the middle of July our equipment had arrived and we were organized as a construction battalion. The order to move out came without warning, we were expected to move instantly and we were not told where we were going. We worked non-stop for 48 hours in pouring rain and knee-deep mud loading aboard Liberty ships. At night we used acetylene construction lights to keep going. By the time we were loaded I was so exhausted that I crawled under a truck aboard the Liberty ship and slept for 18 hours on the steel deck without taking off my boots.

Four days later we landed at our staging area in the middle of the night. In my letters I refer to Maffin Bay on Wakde Island as the staging area but now, from pictures and comments from blogs on the internet, this must have been Biak island. By some miscalculation the damned infantry had not cleared out the Japanese holed up in the cliffs overlooking the beach. The Japanese had mountain howitzers pulled back in caves and would periodically run one out to the mouth of the cave, fire a shell and then pull back into the cave. The Navy shelled the cliffs but the Japanese kept digging out.

Unloading from Liberty Ship

The picture shows loading an LCT with material from a Liberty ship at Biak Island.

In pitch darkness on Biak we were somehow guided to a reasonably flat area to pitch our pup tents in the rain and set up a perimeter. It was an uneasy night, as some idiot would now and then fire his M-1 at nothing. It was dangerous to stand up to urinate.

At day break we moved back to the Liberty ships to offload our trucks, bulldozers and other equipment and supplies to LCVTs, DUKWs and LCTs for transport to shore and from there to LSTs. We worked 24 hours a day and manned the ship winches when the merchant seamen knocked off. We unloaded fast. A cargo net of small items would be unloaded into a DUKW by unhooking a corner of the net and hoisting away to dump the net. Not all of these supplies ended up in the DUKW. After a day and a half we were loaded onto LSTs and away from the Japanese howitzers.

We now learned we were headed for Cape Sansapor on the far western end of New Guinea and the nearby islands of Middleburg and Amsterdam. Supposedly we were bypassing 25,000 Japanese at Manokwari, not far away on the Vogelkop Peninsula, so there was no preliminary bombardment of the landings at Middleburg and Amsterdam on July 29 or of Cape Sansapor on July 30, 1944. However this was our first chance to play infantry and some of the guys in the first wave were so loaded with M-1 clips and hand grenades they would have drowned if they had fallen into the water.

CHAPTER 4
Cape Sansapor

MacArthur, adhering to the principle of avoiding massed enemy concentrations where feasible, advanced to Cape Sansapor and Middleburg and Amsterdam islands 200 miles to the west of Biak and Noemfoor islands which had been subdued by July 22. The airstrips at Sansapor and Middleburg Island not only helped isolate the enemy at Manokwari where the Japanese would die of starvation and disease but these strips also provided air cover for the next advance to Morotai, one of the Halmahera islands.

Initial unopposed landings were on Middleburg and Amsterdam on July 29. On July 30 at the crack of dawn we landed at Cape Sansapor. There was no preliminary bombardment because supposedly there was only empty jungle. The LST was deadly quiet as we approached shore in the dim pre-dawn light. Our memories of Biak Island were fresh in our mind and intelligence had been in error before. Everyone had a clip in his rifle and a few hand grenades hung on his fatigues. The landing was smooth and uneventful. We quickly set up camp under trees that offered camouflage from air raids.

LSTs Lined Up on the Beach After Unopposed Landing at Cape Sansapor

Part of the 1897th went to work with another Aviation Engineering Battalion to build the airstrip on Middleburg Island. This island had been a coconut plantation for a Dutch planter and was a coconut grove on a coral reef. The area was limited but obviously a strip could be quickly constructed by bulldozing off the palm trees and leveling the ground. A larger strip was needed for large bombers that required the space available at Cape Sansapor. Cape Sansapor was flat in a swamp covered with large trees. While the work was rushed on the Middleburg strip for the P-38 fighters the 1897th started clearing jungle at Sansapor.

Airstrip Middleburg Island

Cape Sansapor is where I learned to operate a bulldozer. The sergeant woke me in the middle of the night and said I was going to run Joe's D-8. I asked where Joe was; a tree had fallen on him and fractured his skull.

Davidson on a Caterpillar D-7

The usual procedure for knocking down a large tree with a bulldozer is to first excavate a hole under the down side roots. Then push the dirt to the opposite side of the tree to make a ramp. The you run the bulldozer up the ramp at full speed with the blade raised high to hit as high up the trunk as possible. If the downside hole is deep enough and the upside ramp is high enough the tree goes down. There are hazards to this, especially at night. The impact of the tractor may break off a limb high up in the tree. A ten inch limb falling from a height can be lethal. Another hazard is the vines connecting the trees. An eight or ten inch vine connected to the tree behind you can be strong enough to pull this tree on top of you as you push over the tree in front of your blade.

When the tree starts to fall, you kick the tractor into reverse and back down the ramp as

30

quickly as possible. It is possible for the roots of the falling tree to burst through the ground under the bulldozer and hold it suspended with the tracks whirling in the air. The only way down is to have another tractor pull you off.

Some trees were too large for even a D-8 to knock down. These required tunneling under and blasting down with ammonium nitrate satchel charges ignited with TNT blocks.

Airstrip Clearing Cape Sansapor

*Cape Sansapor Airstrip Before All Trees
Were Cleared*

One night I clipped the side of a rotten tree about four feet in diameter and it fell over on the tractor. The grade foreman yelled a warning to me and I hit the floor of the D-8. The tree disintegrated on hitting the headache bar overhead. The tree was an ant nest, and I was covered from head to foot with inch long ants. Then I was thankful for my long sleeved

32

coveralls buttoned down around the neck. When washing our coveralls we gave them a final rinse in a dimethyl phthalate insect repellent and then hung them up to dry. I did not have a single bite.

The following is my first letter from Sansapor.

New Guinea
Aug 14, 1944

Dear Warren,

This place is slowly becoming civilized. Pretty soon the signs "Speed Limit 20 miles" and MPs will appear.

Last night I attempted to see my first movie in a couple of months. After fully clothing myself, loading my rifle and slinging it over my shoulder and packing a bottle of insect repellant into my pocket I was fully prepared per regulations for attending our theater. The show was "East Side of Heaven" with Bing Crosby and Joan Blondell. After the film breaking a few times things were going smoothly and BINGO - an air raid. That ended, we sat down again, another air raid. The All Clear came and it started pouring rain. It was approaching eleven o'clock and only one reel had been shown so I gave it up. Tomorrow we have another show.

So far in this war I have seen only one dead Jap. He was floating in a river well aged. I have smelt a number though. One of our lieutenants had his carbine taken away for shooting an anteater. The meatballs were unusually good that evening.

I have been running a cat lately on the graveyard shift (we only work 8 hours now) It's a D-8 and weighs twenty some odd tons. Nice machine. Fortunately I have not had to knock down trees. That is bad business, especially at night. No one has been killed yet though.

The "Time" would certainly be appreciated. Most of my news is word of mouth from what somebody heard the first sergeant say he heard on the radio.

Everyone grabs up the "Time" magazines, two and three months old.

I have enclosed a New Guinea shilling. They are rather rare.

Peter

Cape Sansapor is a long way from civilization but life was bearable and we only worked eight hours a day, seven days a week. The air raids were never serious and ceased after the first few weeks. Our camp was on the edge of the beach concealed in the trees. For recreation we had movies, volley ball, baseball and swimming in the ocean. I especially liked the swimming although one encounter with jellyfish made a lasting impression on me. I went dashing through the camp in the nude to the medics.

We had fresh water, showers and soon had a four drum washing machine hooked to the power-take-off of a Ford tractor. Our mechanics and welders made washing machines from oil drums with various sources of power. I remember one powered by a Japanese bicycle and others used a propeller and wind power. Some required manually squooshing a plunger up and down. Not a popular design.

Wind Powered Washing Machines

We saw few animals in the jungle except birds but the animals were shy and there may have been more than we realized. One day we spotted a cuscus up a tree. Not a very active or exciting animal. We were forbidden to shoot animals although you will notice in the August 14 letter that a lieutenant shot an anteater. There were lots of rats of the type in California we call pack rats. They are large and build nests in the trees of twigs. They came in our tents at night and one night an annoyed inmate

shot a rat under a tent-mate's cot with a
Tommy gun. He caught hell for that.

   We did not venture into the jungle much but
we would go if we heard of banana trees or a
papaya tree that had not been stripped. With
spurs I learned to climb coconut trees for fresh
coconuts. The meat of the fallen coconuts is
good but the fresh coconuts have the only
drinkable milk.

Native Village at Cape Sansapor

   One night we had a band play a concert
around a big bonfire. Out of the darkness came
the natives to squat around the band and beat
their hands in rhythm. They had come right
through our perimeter without being seen.
When the concert was over they disappeared
again into the darkness. There were natives in

this area that had never seen white men before and believed airplanes were gods.

The natives in the Sansapor area were quite different from the natives of Papua. The contact with people from outside New Guinea had been limited. Apparently there were no missionaries in this part of New Guinea.

B-24 Bomber Emergency Landing Middleburg Island

The strip on Middleburg Island was usable in only two weeks because the island was a flat coconut plantation and there was coral for the sub-grade. The Dutch plantation owner's house was on neighboring Amsterdam Island, also a coconut plantation. The picture above shows the first B-24 bomber landing in an emergency.

Sansapor Air Base Cleared of Trees, Ready for Sub-grade

The Sansapor location had the advantage of being flat with plenty of room to expand into a bomber base. One problem was the large trees, some too large for the bulldozers to handle without being blasted down and sawed into smaller pieces. Sometimes we would line up D-8s and D-7s along a large tree trunk and move it off in one piece.

1897th Camp Area

Cape Sansapor Bomber Base Completed

The water was handled with drainage ditches but you cannot build a bomber strip on sand. Steel landing mat will not last long if it is not laid on a firm sub-grade. Hauling the coral gravel in for the strip and taxiway sub-grade required all the trucks, Turnapulls and carryalls available. After the trees had been cleared we removed the blades from most of the D-8s and D-7 tractors and hooked them to carryalls for hauling coral.

In the picture above (taken from a Piper Cub) you can see the operational strip is a dark color because the steel matting is laid over asphalt sealed coral with dark aprons on each side of asphalt sealed coral. Parallel to the strip is the first taxiway with hard stands of asphalt sealed coral but no landing mat. Beyond the first taxiway is another taxiway with hard stands under construction. These are of white coral that has not been sealed yet.

Sansapor was an important base for P-38 fighters and B-25 and B-24 bombers. Just above the wing of the Piper Cub you can see a B-24, two B-25s and a P-38. With the elimination of nearby Japanese Zero fighters the P-38 fighters were used mostly as bombers against Japanese shipping in the East Indies and the Philippines. B-25s, some with a 75mm cannon in the nose also went after shipping. The B-24 heavy bombers concentrated on enemy airfields and helped prepare the way for the landings on Moratai in the Halmahera group of islands.

We had a sawmill but most of the local trees were softwood that was not strong and rotted within weeks. For good timbers to build bridges we looked for mahogany trees. This was my introduction to the use of a chain saw. Mahogany trees grow individually in the jungle, not in groves. I would go through the jungle with my machete until I found a tree one or two feet in diameter. I would cut this down and find someone with a bulldozer to drag the tree to the sawmill. We used green logs; we did not have time to let them cure. A mahogany bridge is a substantial structure.

The following are my letters of September 2 and September 8 1944.

Sept. 2, 1944
New Guinea

Dear Warren,

My big trouble with answering letters is that I can't answer them immediately after reading them. Consequently if I write you without first rereading your letter I forget to answer your questions. At any rate the bulky letter with clipping have been coming through in twelve to fifteen days while the light ones take up to a month

I have enclosed a "Guinea Gold" which we manage to get a copy of about once a month. Also you should find some invasion money in the letter. I am not allowed to send Dutch money.

I write on both sides of the paper because it is scarce. I hope the censor does not cut it up too much. Incidentally meet the censor Lt. Sells—Mr. Manter.

I am back to knocking down trees again. You should see the ants. Almost an inch long! We are building a road along the side of a hill so steep that last night two cats walked out of their tracks.

Tokyo Rose has been promising us all sorts of things but so far our sleep is about the only thing that has been bothered and also our movies. I am becoming tired of—this place—too civilized now.

Keep sending maps. I managed to listen to a radio now and then but the names don't mean much. In the last bunch to arrive I discovered that I was on the edge of the black area. Give my regards to everyone.
    Peter

Bulldozing The Way From New Guinea To Japan

Sept. 8, 1944
New Guinea
Dear Warren,

Number 33 arrived the fifth. That is about the usual time. Clippings are as fast as letters.

Now for a few questions. It may be warm in the daytime but it is cool at night. I always sleep under a blanket which is more than one can say for Virginia.

What I get to read may be of any age depending on whether it was flown in the same day as it was published or was carried on a boat for six months.

I am not allowed to tell you any place I have been in since I left Richmond but you know where I am now. You mentioned it in your last V-Mail. Also your friend cannot be any farther up than I am.

We have movies three times a week (nothing less than two years old) and the radio in Company Headquarters is close by. The trouble is getting the station you want. Once in a while I managed to find one without someone twirling its dial. Some of these propaganda broadcasts are pretty good. I usually listen to Radio Saigon and Tokyo Rose has specifically promised us many things including gas but the P-61 or Black Widows have disposed of our little friends. They had a hidden airfield near here that required a month to find.

PX, libraries and floors are foreign words. Our sawmill is going full blast but we will never bother with floors.

Typhus, dengue, malaria, jungle rot and ringworm are the main diseases but any figures are strictly verboten. Last night I slept on a cot with a rent down the middle. I hope to get a jungle hammock some day. A large collection of land crabs and lizards share our tent with us.

Petrokowitz told me to tell you that he resents being referred to as a Pole. He is Russian. He works as a mechanic now.

Perhaps I told you before but the medics had all their clinical thermometers broken by the heat when we first moved in here.

We have certainly changed this place in a month. It is hard to believe that where P-38's come roaring in I was knocking down trees and filling in a swamp a short while ago. (with a dozer of course)

> Peter

I thought of something else. An infantry fellow was telling me that at Wakde there is a concrete fortification the Japs dated 1935 and at Maffin Bay the Japs had a drill field and held maneuvers in 1939.

Petrokowitz was a longshoreman from Brooklyn, Russian parents. Petrok was one of the more articulate members of our heavy equipment platoon, which had more than its share of outspoken critics of the army, the officers and the non-coms. For some reason the two of us hit it off in spite of our differences in education and background.

Living in the jungle was not like living in France or Italy. Certain basic soldier interests did not exist such as beer halls or laundry facilities. Making jungle juice was the answer to the lack of beer halls. Here are detailed instructions on making jungle juice.

Making Jungle Juice

1. Fermentation Vat. Half of a 55 gallon oil drum is enough for a single batch. Notice the sticks for stirring. What is not shown is the cloth covering to keep out the insects that converge on anything fermenting. The insects do not affect the flavor but they are unattractive and may promote the fermentation of vinegar. The essential ingredients are sugar and water and then fruit, raisins, papayas, coconut juice and any fruit, canned or fresh, to supply the necessary enzymes, acid and yeast

44

to initiate fermentation. A bit of baker's yeast is a big help. In tropical climates ten days fermentation is enough before distillation.

2. Boiler. A five gallon jerry can. Looks like this is a gasoline jerry can with a screw top and a small vent for attaching the copper tube vapor line.

3. Heat. The source of heat appears to be a regular army stove of the type used to boil water and coffee in 30 gallon galvanized garbage cans.

4. Vapor Line. The overhead vapor line appears to be a piece of ¼ inch copper tubing. This would have been difficult to obtain in New Guinea. After the 1897th inherited a Japanese truck supply caravan the infantry captured on Route 2 from Dulag, Leyte, an assortment of hardware was available.

5. Condenser. Half of a 55 gallon oil drum with the copper line coiled inside makes an adequate condenser. The water must be manually replaced to keep it cool. Note the water can on the left for this purpose.

6. Spigot on end of copper coil protruding from side of condenser drum.

7. Coke bottle to receive juice from condenser.

8. First sample of "juice" hot from condenser.

The fermentation yield of alcohol from these primitive facilities was probably 8 to 9 volume percent (16 to 18 proof) . Thus a five gallon batch would contain about 51 liquid ounces of 100 proof alcohol. 80% of this would come over in the first two gallons distilled to give a liquid 31 proof. The first few ounces of alcohol distilled packed quite a wallop and contained various aldehydes and esters that promote blindness and other afflictions. The "first run" two gallons needed redistilling to produce about 100 ounces (about 3 quarts) of 80 proof alcohol after discarding the first few ounces containing the aldehydes. This yield sounds high for these facilities. Maybe you could produce two quarts of drinkable stuff from five gallons of mash.

The pictured equipment was often unattainable so we would settle for a simple fermentation. The simplest was to drill a hole in a green coconut, stuff in sugar, raisins, papaya or canned fruit. Plug and place under your cot. When the plug blew out it was ready to drink.

The best material for wine was canned pie cherries. A couple of gallon cans of pie cherries in a water jerry can with sugar and water would produce drinkable wine, especially if was aged a month or more. The only time our wine was permitted to age was during the confusion of the Leyte invasion. We placed the jerry can in the tool box of the ditching machine and did not have access to the ditching machine for six weeks.

Life at Cape Sansapor was becoming too easy. The air strip, taxiways and hard stands were built and in use. We had some beer rations, not much work to do and suddenly we were rifle practicing, using bazookas and practicing with mortars. Obviously something was going to happen soon.

The following are letters of September 20, 1944. Inez is Warren's wife.

New Guinea
Sept. 20, 1944
Dear Inez,

You are quite correct about causing my mouth to water. The last home cooked meal at the Manters' is a fond memory. However I have been having a little luck on the food situation lately. One fellow in my tent receives packages of canned chicken, turkey, cheese and fruit. His father owns a grocery store in New York. Another fellow hauls rations, taking his cut of course. Also my mother sent some candy and I have been doing some procuring myself. One day I found a bunch of good bananas while bulldozing down jungle, and the next day I received twelve bottles of beer for doing some work for an ack-ack outfit. The beer itself does not interest me, but it is the best currency in New Guinea. Last night I cleared jungle for the Quartermaster Corp which netted me a few cans of fruit cocktail.

Last week one of the most unusual things happened to me since I joined the army. I spent the morning laying a concrete floor for an ack-ack outfit. When I finished the lieutenant not only handed me a few bottles of beer but also a 10 guilder ($5.30) tip. I almost fainted.

Say hello to the Leshes for me. I'll always appreciate their hospitality last Christmas. Also give my regards to Carolyn if she is there.

Peter

New Guinea
Sept. 20, 1944

Dear Warren,

This past week every letter through number 42 has arrived. No exceptional speed. Fourteen to sixteen days for all of them.

Thanks for the coin although I doubt if I will ever land there. The reason the shilling was so shiny is that only the natives have them (hence the hole for tying them together). They never spend them but store them away in the New Guinea equivalent of the old sock. With the arrival of the Americans the little hijackers have made a good profit trading the New Guinea shillings for two Australian. 100% profit.

The magazine I should prefer is the "Readers' Digest." I will really appreciate it. The sixteenth the first issue (Aug 14) of "Time" arrived. That is good time for ordinary mail and it is the latest magazine in camp.

The clippings have really been welcome lately because I haven't been able to listen to the radio.

The advent of beer has really made every one happy around here. We have a refrigerator trailer that keeps the battalion supply cold. Most outfits have to cool them by wrapping the bottles in cloths soaked with aviation gasoline which cools by evaporation.

Our food is somewhat better with regular air transport in now. There is a continual thunder of airplanes all day and all night. I'll be glad when we move but God knows when that will be.

Tell Bennett the writing on the coin was Malay.

Peter

The bazooka practice was unnerving. The electrical firing system of a bazooka was not designed to last very long in a hot, humid climate. I remember once I used the test light on my bazooka and it appeared OK. I tried firing and nothing happened. I kept trying to fire and nothing happened. I unwound the firing wire and laid the bazooka down. The rocket went off, skittering and bouncing over the ground. Fortunately it did not hit anything to set it off.

The 60mm mortars are a professional weapon. It is obvious that with practice a team can learn to place a shell accurately on target. Using a mortar in the jungle can be tricky. The shell must have a clear field of fire because if it hits even a leaf on the way up it will explode. The infantry is welcome to their toys.

The following are the last three letters written in New Guinea.

New Guinea
Sept. 28, 1944

Dear Warren.

Airmail number 43 arrived today. I saw the map in battalion headquarters and know where I am but it still does not have a name just APO 159. Your map will be welcome. Also you might dig up a few pictures, snapshots or what have you of the family.

Watch the news of this area closely now. They are actually giving furloughs to Australia now but I doubt if I have much chance.

When did you get all these ideas about DDT? We have to keep our sleeves rolled down and wear leggings at all times. Also no mixed uniforms – i.e., fatigue pants and suntan shirt.

I have been operating a grader, keeping the road in shape. Very boring.

However, life has been so pleasant as it will ever be in N. G. Bunch of bananas hanging up in the tent, a collection of books and magazines and not much work to do.

The rainy season is with us; cool but hard to get your clothes dry.

Take it from me; the Japs are really catching lots of bombs these days. I wish I could elucidate.

My mother sent me a pipe with a red stem to trade with the natives. I figured it would be good for two bunches of bananas, but the boys in the tent have appropriated it.

As ever, Peter

N.G,
Oct 5, 1944

Dear Warren,

Your S.E.P. arrived in perfect condition and not one had seen them. Also the book "Turning Wheels" which I have not had time to read yet. No. 74 + V-mail 61 arrived 2 days ago; this letter + Jan. 18 today. The talcum powder works fine.

Back on a dozer again. For a while I worked at the gravel pit pushing gravel off a 75 embankment with no brakes. Boy. How the sun beats down and reflects off those rocks! Good job today working at the hospital. I hear medics live like kings – mess halls concrete floors and even tables to eat at + ice water to drink. I am building a road to the top of the steepest and tallest hill the medics could find. They are going to build a recreation hall there. You arrive at too many logical conclusions - thought you were in the army 16 years.

N. G.
Oct. 10, 1944

Dear Warren,

  The quality of N.G. writing paper is declining as you can see. Letters through 45 including two without a number came through all right. 45 & one of the others arrived in 10 and 11 days respectively.

  I have been practicing with my rifle, a bazooka and 60 mm mortar. Boy does that mortar lay them in there. One of these days I hope to see some signs of civilization. Do you realize that it has been six months since I have seen a white man's house?

  A Lt. who flies a P38 out of this field was in to see me the other day. His wife rooms with my sister. These boys really go through something.

This is all for now.

Peter

  Finally the day came. Off again in LSTs, three for our battalion. We were not told, of course, but we were headed for Leyte in the Philippines to build an airfield for MacArthur. Our scheduled landing was October 24 at Dulag, south of Tacloban on Leyte.

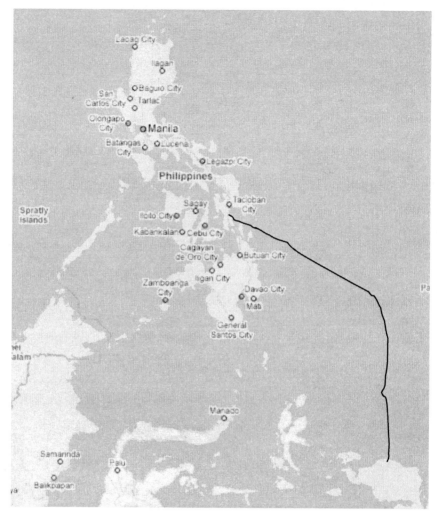

Map 3 - Cape Sansapor to Dulag, Leyte.

CHAPTER 5
Leyte

October 24, 1944, the 1897th landed at Dulag, Leyte, in a fog of smoke from constant 40 mm and 20 mm canon firing at Japanese planes overhead.

What we did not know was that this was the day of the big attack by the Japanese fleet to wipe out the landing. The Japanese attacked with some of their largest ships and Halsey and the bulk of his force had gone chasing a decoy Japanese fleet. The only naval forces left to protect the Leyte landing were escort carriers, destroyers and PT boats. The Japanese battleships, cruisers and destroyers soon sank some escort carriers and the Navy planes were looking for a place to land. The Tacloban strip became overcrowded with planes so the Navy planes started landing on the Dulag strip. This was a Japanese built strip, covered with grass turf, barely suitable for lightweight Japanese planes and good only for emergency landings by heavy American planes.

I remember one Lt. Commander landing his fighter plane there. The plane bogged down in the mud and it was obviously impossible to take off again. On top of this, the U.S. anti-aircraft gunners were shooting at anything that flew, including American planes. That was one irate Lt. Commander that climbed out of his fighter plane.

Children swimming to our LST at Dulag

The Filipinos in the Dulag area swarmed to the beach to greet the Americans which complicated the landing and anti-aircraft flak problems.

Each LST had a D-8 bulldozer equipped for underwater operation. This bulldozer landed first and built a ramp for all the other equipment to land from the LST. To the left in the picture on page 54 is the bulldozer with the beginning of the ramp.

Filipinos Greeting Our Landing at Dulag

The Filipino children came swimming around in front of the LST ramp and a bulldozer that was building up a sand ramp for landing.

Fortunately, no one was injured. The Filipinos crowded the beaches to welcome us even though Zeros were strafing and the flak from the anti-aircraft shells was dangerous.

The Japanese had resisted strongly at Dulag and had sent two tanks down Route 2. The American offensive with the Navy shelling was overwhelming; the tanks were knocked out and the Japanese pushed inland.

The Leyte landings were made at the beginning of the rainy season. MacArthur should have known this since Tacloban had been his first assignment in the Philippines as a second lieutenant. Later, General Kenney, MacArthur's air chief of staff, blamed himself for trying to rebuild the Japanese airfields in the mud during the continuous downpour.

Route 2 from Dulag to the front was jammed with vehicles trying to get through the mud. I was on a motor grader trying to keep Route 2 open. I had an armed guard with me as protection against snipers. Once a Zero caught me and I dove under the grader. Fortunately the machine gun bullets went on both sides of me but I will always remember staring into the face of the Japanese pilot.

We camped in the jungle next to Route 2 and the airfields. It was too wet for foxholes so we slept in jungle hammocks and hoped no enemy with bayonets would find us in the night.

We could not build an airstrip so we played infantry, going on patrols and searching for snipers whom we did not find. We also observed the professionals of the First Cavalry in action. The rule was do not send in the infantry if the artillery can do it better. The infantry would locate the Japanese strong points, the artillery would send over a Piper Cub observation plane and initially the 105 mm

Our Lady of Refuge Church at Dulag Was Not Spared

howitzers would zero in on the Japanese. If the 105s were not effective, the 155 mm Long Toms would take over. Then the infantry would clean up the mess.

The following is my first letter from the Philippines.

Philippines
October 1944

Dear Warren,

There is nothing to write about but at least you will have my new APO (705). Did they cut much out of my last letter? No one said anything but I am not sure. At any rate I'll be somewhere when you receive this and you should be able to figure out where.

Nothing to do but lounge around, eat and read. "Turning Wheels" is quite a book. I think I am gaining weight. We've had a little action. It may get through the censorship in six months or so.

I sleep in a jungle hammock stretched between a jeep and a truck. I prefer a hammock to these backbreaking GI cots. Three of us have trucks roofed with a couple of ponchos for a place to read & write. It is not a bad trip. The navy certainly has the edge on the army in respect to chow.

Give my regards to Inez & the kids.

Peter

In the jungle Cossack guard was necessary to establish a perimeter around our company. Guard posts were set up two hand grenade throws apart and we were forbidden to use rifles unless there was a major attack. A guard post consisted of three men, one with a stack of grenades while the other two tried to sleep on the ground in ponchos. The problem was that all the insects around wanted out of the rain also and they crawled in with you. Standing Cossack guard was not comfortable.

The following is my second letter written in the Philippines.

Philippines
Oct. 30,1944

Dear Warren,

You are much better acquainted with the news from here than I am so there no use going into details.

However, I never saw anyone happier than the Filipinos who greeted us on the beach. They were in a pretty bad way with no clothes, no food and their villages leveled from shellfire. You could not eat a C-biscuit without being surrounded by everyone from naked little kids to grandmothers. Petrokowitz rode around on the fender of a truck throwing cans of food to every pretty girl who smiled at him.

I'm writing this sitting upon the edge of my cot ankle deep in mud. If there is no mud you can hardly breathe for the dust. We are in a continuous air alert with more raids than you can bother to count. We never even look up unless the Zeros head in our direction. Yesterday afternoon I had a good scare when about ten Zeros came down to strafe the strip and concentrated on the motor pool where I was cranking a grader. Did I dive under it in a hurry? They have shot down a lot of planes but the news I heard the other night over the radio in our half-track about 56 planes being knocked down here in one day is a lot of baloney,

We have Filipino boys in our tent that we feed and clothe and they dig our ditches and foxholes, sets up mosquito boxes, bring in bananas and so forth. Next to find a girl to do my washing. About a hundred feet away is a Jap tank whose occupants no one has bothered to scrape out. If the wind blows in our direction too much we'll have to burn out the tank.

I have been running a motor grader up and down the road with a man beside me with a rifle to watch for snipers. Haven't been bothered though. If the Sea Bees get all the credit for the strips here don't believe it.
Peter

Finally the top brass realized that it was impossible to build an airfield out of mud. We were moved to the beach at Tanauan and started to build the Tanauan airfield out of sand and coral. In the meantime other engineering battalions had commenced construction of airfields on the island of Mindoro for the support of landings on Luzon. Mindoro was much drier than Leyte.

The location at Tanauan was pleasant, on the beach under palm trees with sand under foot. I was working nights running a boiler for the asphalt plant. I would be off work early in the morning, have a swim and then turn in to catch up on my sleep. The Filipino girls would come around and take our laundry. The price was modest but they preferred a loaf of bread or some sugar.

Airstrip Built at Tanauan by the 1897th

The families sent the girls around to drum up business but the older women actually did the work with the GI soap we supplied.

Washing Clothes in a Stream

Laundry Girls

Philippines
Early in November, 1944

(note: The first part of this letter was torn in half by the censor and this is the bottom half of the page, front and back.)

I received three of your airmails a few days ago and yesterday four airmails arrived. 10-10, 10-7 and clippings. The latest V-mail is 46. V-mail is lousy here.

A canvas writing case would be good. The one my mother gave me has fallen apart. It also had an ant's nest in it. This climate is hell on anything.

Rain, rain, rain. I never saw so much in my life. Our equipment is immobilized.

(note: Top half of back page was torn off by the censor. The first remaining line starts in the middle of a sentence and obviously refers to our laundry girls.)

.... around for laundry dressed in their best dresses. What a line some of them have!
Don't worry about the "Posts" being too old. I just finished one dated May 20.

I have been running a grader and a ditcher. Nothing exciting. Lots of nuisance raids but we do not pay any attention to them. We are not the main target. I hope everyone is well and so forth. Radio Tokyo is playing "It's a Long, Long Way from Home"

Peter

 ←   Philippine mud

Tuba Salesman

To drink there was tuba, palm wine scooped from the top of palm trees. The Filipinos could not understand why we objected to the wine being full of bugs and flies but they finally learned to filter the stuff before selling it to the Americans.

Philippines
Dec. 24, 1944

Dear Warren,

Our air raids seem to be over for the evening so I'll finally get off a letter to you. Censor trouble lately. The last was returned. P-38's have certainly been doing the victory rolls lately.

Big day today. I received the first letters in weeks, a package containing an edible fruitcake and six bottles of beer. Your "Posts" arrived the other day. They had evidently been soaked in seawater and then vigorously tramped upon but they are legible. However I would not suggest repeating the experiment.

This talk about stamps refers to Philippine stamps I presume. They are very difficult to get.

I have "Time" sent airmail now. That along with your clippings is the latest printed news here. I pass them around and everyone enjoys them.

Your guesses are about as close as could be expected within 15 miles anyway. However that once I was on a grader, not a bulldozer.

We are now camped upon the beach in the best area we have had. Sand and not mud thank God.

In the other letters I extensively answered all your previous letters but since it was returned I will not try that again.

The shells in the bracelet are cowry shells I guess. The boy who writes upon the shells must have made a fortune. He charges a guilder (peso) a shell.

Number 61 arrived today, 57 dated No. 14 is the latest before that. I presume you have settled down by now. Be thankful that you have not the thousands of tons of scrap iron to take care of that we have.

Peter

The children would come to our chow lines with cans and instead of emptying our mess kits into the garbage can we would empty them into their cans.

Filipino Children

Once again living became pleasant, the air strip was functioning and we had a beer ration. It was obvious we were going to move.

Church of the Assumption at Tanauan

The Church of the Assumption was pictured in Time magazine. By referring to this picture in my letter to Warren I was able to tell him my location on Leyte. This church is still in use at Tanauan but it is now surrounded by schools and other buildings.

Philippines
Jan. 8,1945

Dear Warren,
Don't sneer too much at the cabarets here. The Japs provide the soldiers better entertainment than the city of Richmond did – at a price, of course but we chisel it back on the black market.

Could tell some choice things about these paratroopers but when I tried, my letter was returned. You can limit your news columns to suit your discretion now because "Time" gets here almost as fast as your letters. The maps and pictures are always welcome. Letter number 67 is the latest and the back letters have caught up.

I have seen the church in that picture in "Time" frequently. I hope to be able to take some pictures soon if my film arrives.

This outfit has gotten a craze for checkers! Damndest thing I ever heard of.

My suspicion grows daily. The food is surprisingly good, movies almost every night, not too much work and we even have a day room (some of the boys swiped a large tent) with books and magazines. Mark my words, this altruism has something nasty behind it.

Tell Bennett to expect a box in the next two or three months.

Much to my amazement I received two or three fruitcakes in good condition. From the soaked and battered condition of most packages they had been used in place of sand bags to build up ramps to LST's to let an armored division ashore.

Some of the boys had invitations to dinner Christmas and New Years. I didn't but we had good dinners.

I really appreciated the envelopes but please put talcum powder on the gummed edges.

I've been busy explaining to dim witted looeys how to build hard stands and taxi ways. Also run a grader.
Peter

Philippines
Jan. 17,1945

Dear Warren,

Letters dated Nov. 20, 19, and 21 arrived today. Latest letter is No.70 dated Jan 4 arrived three days ago. Incidentally I have a good supply of airmail envelopes but I can always use the paper — very scarce here. I am very well acquainted with the airstrips mentioned in that clipping. Censorship won't allow me to say anything about Jap Paratroopers in connection with that. However, in fact I would not even be allowed to send back some of the clippings that you send me!

What stamps do you want? Surely not on the envelopes that you send me. It is impossible to buy Philippine stamps.

It was raining so hard today I could not see whether my grader blade was touching the ground or not so I got under the wing of a plane. The major came by and - to paraphrase an old army saying he masticated my posterior thoroughly.

I received a letter from Bennett. The lad is nuts- I'll never forget the morning I woke up in a pup tent with my feet out in the snow - the first time I had ever seen snow. (same tent I think).

This place bores me although I know the next place will be worse. I swim from half a mile to a mile about every day now. KP Manana. Give my regards to Inez and the rest of the family.

Good night
Peter

P.S. I save your large envelopes for my correspondence course reports. Also your candy arrived yesterday in edible condition. Other fellows in the tent received canned fried chicken, cake and cookies. Did we eat!! Readers Digest came today also, the maps a couple of weeks ago. Very good.

Road Built by the 1897th Near Tanauan

The 1897th built roads as well as airstrips.

Philippines
Jan 30,1945

Dear Warren,

Your letter of Jan 18 arrived yesterday and two V-Mails 59 & 68 arrived a week ago. V-Mail isn't much good here. Has to be developed in Moresby. That is a good story about PBY's. These fighter pilots swear by them. Same old thing here - grader work and rain. Not much chance of a change either since we are out of the Sixth Army and in Service Forces. Pain in the neck. We are treated like an unwanted child the way we are transferred from one branch to another of the Army. I'll be glad when it stops raining. Our tent only slows down the water. I'd wear my raincoat to bed if I had a raincoat. You can cut down on the news reviews with "Time" coming through.
Peter

Questionnaire enclosed.

3215 Monument Avenue 4
Richmond 20 Virginia.

January 20 1945.

Dear Peter;

QUESTIONNAIRE,

1. Is that beach where you are camped hard or soft? *Soft*

2. Can you go In swimming? *Yes*

3. Do you? *Yes – when I wasn't working hard, ½ to a mile a day.*

4. Why not?

5 What did the Filipinos feed the men that they asked out for Christmas dinner? *Rice, pork (whole pig), chicken, eggs, sweet and white potatoes and weird dishes they were afraid to ask about.*

6. Has your day room tent got a floor? *No.*

7. Who supplies the books and magazines? *Red Cross*

8. How many books are there, 10 or 100? *none*

9. How many different magazines? *Life, S.E.P. (Saturday Evening Post), Infantry J., I.D.A.*

10. What are they

11. What is in the box that Bennett will get? *Wait and find out.*

12. Did you ever get that famous map? Mailed September 7. Bad mistake to send it ordinary mail. (It was a big National Geographic map of the Asiatic Area). *Yes, thought I told you. Good map, everyone uses it. Hope I get it back.*

Theater at Tanauan

When this theater was built we knew were moving soon. The Heavy Equipment Platoon had their picture taken before boarding the LST.

Third Platoon, 1897th Headquarters Company

72

CHAPTER 6
Palawan

We boarded LSTs, stopped at Mindoro and then sailed for Puerto Princessa, Palawan.

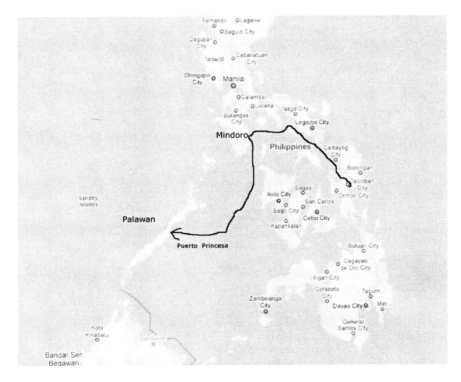

Map 4 - Tanauan to Puerto Princessa, Palawan

We landed at Puerto Princessa at 4 AM February 27 after a heavy bombardment.

A Japanese Zero on the Edge of the Puerto Princessa Air Strip

This was a Japanese Zero the way we liked to see them. We discovered that the Japanese were using ethyl alcohol as fuel for their planes and all the aviation fuel drums we found were full of alcohol that was not heavily denatured. We soon had over twenty of our construction experts in the hospital with alcohol poisoning. However, you could drink a small amount of this fuel without serious effects.

Philippines
Feb.6, 1945

Dear Warren,

As you have doubtlessly read things are under control here
and everything is proceeding according to plan – if there is any.

This island is much drier, hotter and yet does not seem as
tropical. Sparsely populated and very little under cultivation. I
have not seen any natives yet to speak to. There are not any rice
paddies so evidently rice is not the main food as on you know
where. Citrus trees grow here as well as quite a few pineapples. I
don't suppose the oranges are any good but the lemons and
limes are okay.

Until I hit this place I had not realized the effect of bombing
and shelling. You should have seen it at first! The strips and such
were churned into shambles. I'll try to send you pictures of what
happened to the Jap air force.

The Japs are certainly expert at camouflage. Even the roads
leading to supply dumps are lined with trees and covered with
grass so that I doubt if they are visible from the air.

I think I told you that the writing paper and kit arrived. My
mother sent some film so I'll try to send you some pictures.
Peter

Philippines
March 25

Dear Warren,

More mail than I know what to do with! Letters 81,83,80,84,
85 and 86 today, not to mention many from other people. It is a
waste of time writing you because you know more about where I
am and what I am doing than I do. The laundry situation is
terrible. I believe if I can find a Filipino girl I'll go as far as to
marry her.

Most of the Moros are down south but beyond that all your information is correct. We ran aground coming in. What the papers euphemistically termed airstrips were a hell of a mess. The Air Corps went farther than was necessary. Your LST surmise is absolutely correct. Of course I still have the hammock. Swiped it from the quartermaster Infantry equipment.

I wrote you about the Jap paratroopers. The censor and I went round and round. Fortunately I did not see them nor they me. I had to destroy the letter.

I think I could make money by starting a circulating library with my "Time" issues.

Concerning the Moros here is a little story a Filipino sergeant of the guerillas told to me. Down on Mindanao the bunch of Moros he was with captured a plump Japanese captain. They were celebrating their victory by getting nicely decorated on tuba when the idea occurred to alleviate the meat shortage by the time honored method of their ancestors. So they put the captain on a spit and dined on "long pig."

Your comments on the carbine are correct. The infantry threw the damn popguns away on Guinea. Me for an M1. Which reminds me, the last place I was at on NG has been given back to the Japs. I am not squeamish but that is a dirty trick to play even on a Jap.

I see in the March 12 issue of "Time" the reference to the occupants of the hundred and some odd graves I dug. Fortunately a hole 18 inches wide and 2 ft long and 3' deep was sufficient. Even with a ditching machine grave digging is tough work in this soil. My God what a stench. No Jap prisoners on this island.

Lexington is a very attractive town to live in according to one of the fellows in my tent.
Peter

Philippines
April 7, 1945

Dear Warren,

Number 90 came this noon, mailed March 27th. Eleven days is fast moving. Bink received one letter from me in six days. I also have 88 and 89, which arrived a few days ago. The package with the socks got through and did I need them. The army is stingy with socks. I thought I had mentioned them.

Nothing new to write about. Dug a half-mile of five-foot ditch for the signal corps. You have to grease that damn ditcher every two hours, continually fill it with gas, oil and water, check two transmissions, four gear boxes and aircleaner once a week and usually flush them out. There are 125 grease fittings on it. One of these days I'll pack the toolbox with TNT and spread that Rube Goldberg invention all over the island. You also have to take the carburetor apart at least once a week.

Yes, I'd like whatever you have to read and can send conveniently. Is that enough for the post office? I cannot find your written request. Also about the magazine you wanted to send, either "New Yorker" or "Comet" would be good. February 'Readers' Digest' came April 1 which is good time.

If you have noticed: our time limit for one location is around three months. During that time we build a strip, roads, hospitals and warehouse, bridges and docks. I can't see how we can finish here in that time but? quien sabe? Working for B Company today, the only men they could spare to clear brush from in front of the ditcher were a first looey and the first sergeant. I sat down and watched them.

The pineapples usually get picked when they are half ripe. I could have told you about the Ryukyu invasions a month before it happened but thought it was only a rumor. Seventeen more months to go. Remember the floors? Had to tear them out 2 weeks ago.

Peter.
April 17, 1945
The Philippines

Dear Bennett,
It seems that I owe you a couple of letters; I had better catch up. The bolo is a common, garden variety; I tried to get hold of a fancy one with hand carved mahogany case but no luck. It is

worn on the left side like a sword or bayonet. The Filipino blacksmiths collect steel, especially spring steel, to make bolos.

Some of the boys had floors in their tents for a couple of days and then they took them away. I have a concrete platform beside my bed, which they will have to blast to get. At any rate, we built a good mess hall right away instead of waiting until about two weeks before we move.

We have two puppies and a monkey in camp that really raise hell. The monkey got into the dentist tools the other day and spread them all over the area.

I thought your father was joking when he talked about buying a woman but there is a village about forty miles from here where you can buy a wife for twelve pesos. Of course, it isn't the initial cost but the upkeep.

Your father wrote that you are going up in the world – assistant scoutmaster now.

We are getting beer again. It is a good thing; some of the G.I.'s have been drinking a mixture of alcohol, ether and other things the Japs used in their planes. Thanks for writing and say hello to your mother, father and sister for me.

Peter

Philippines
April 29, 1945

Dear Warren,

Your clipping of Roosevelt, a letter dated April 1 and number 94 came the last few days. I have a few things to report for a change.

Among other things one fellow was clipped in the seat of the pants trying to outrun a daisy cutter. We got quite a laugh out of it and he is going to have a tough time explaining his purple heart.

Has this page been torn in two? I won't write on the other side.

We start working twelve hours shifts tomorrow running from midnight to noon, noon to midnight. Maybe they will get more work out of us but I doubt it. Today I was digging a ditch in the nurses' quarter and the ditcher jumped out of time and clogged its carburetor. I suppose I'll get it out of there eventually.

A week ago by devious and illegal methods I had a day off. A bunch of us got hold of a DUKW* and went fishing using TNT & dynamite for tackle. Four sticks of dynamite or two blocks of TNT do an effective job. Part of the fish floated to the top; the others we had to dive for on the bottom. Our catch ranged from a three-foot catfish to a forty or fifty small sea trout and perch plus a few large pompanos. These were the best foods I have tasted in a long time.

Have you been able to figure out our next operation? I have a sneaking suspicion the 8th army is going to mop up all the God forsaken holes that exist in this part of the world.

Sincerely yours,
Peter P.S. It's too hot for candy. Thanks anyway.
*A DUKW is a 6x6 2-1/2 ton amphibious truck.

New Letter
(Page 1 thrown away by censor.)

The hammock is only for emergencies.

If my mother sends you the pictures she is supposed to, you will see how I live – same as always on a canvas cot in a pyramidal tent, six man. Incidentally, the hammock is equipped with waterproof cover and mosquito netting. Once you zip yourself in, you pray that you don't have to get out in a hurry. Sometimes during nightmares you will turn upside down lying in the rain shelter, the hammock above and the mosquito netting slowly strangling you. The only solution is to cut your way out with a trench knife.

Reading between the lines of the news reports I should say that the brass has made the same mess on Okinawa that they made on Leyte in airfield construction.

In case I did not mention it, a daisy cutter is a 1 lb to 2 lb fragmentation bomb that is not as dangerous as a hand grenade but is still very uncomfortable if it blows you out of bed. I'll try to send you one.

We are back on eight-hour shifts. Thirty per cent loss in efficiency the other way.

The Philippine army has taken over from the infantry. Never were many Japs here and I doubt if any prisoners were taken.

The beach is a mile away and full of coral reefs. To go swimming you have to go out in a boat. I guess there are no sharks in these parts. I have swum a half-mile or so from shore and I have swum from boats much farther out. I have yet to encounter barracuda or sharks.

51 discharge points are all I can manage, a long way from 85. They have started sending the 42 year olds home.

The mechanics dream up lots of washing machines but someone confiscates the motors eventually. I finally found a Filipino to take care of my laundry at ceiling prices.
The mess in the picture is now a taxiway. Fortunately none of duds exploded. Damn this writing on my lap.

Peter

May 7, 1945
Philippines
Dear Warren,

Number 96 and 97 are the latest. Day before yesterday I believe. None of your letters have been censored to date. They spot-check very little incoming mail.

I think I mentioned that you can buy a wife for twelve pesos. The police chief of this town about forty miles away is the retailer. The rub is that she has to be supported in a house in a decent style and it costs a lot of money to trade an old wife in on a newer model.

We have not been allowed to mention the "Special Attack Corps" that Radio Manila use to advertise so widely but I see that it has finally come out in "Time". That is what those paratroopers were. They may not be very efficient but they are nasty to tangle with.

Any reading material you have to send I would like. Especially see if you cannot find a "World Almanac" new enough to contain the 1940 census. We are always having arguments that we cannot settle.

This place is beginning to pall. They even make you tuck in your shirttail now. I am looking forward to June. I am still in the ditching business. I ran the ditcher into a five-foot hole the other day. It took a ten-ton wrecker and a D-8 bulldozer to get me out.

Peter

Philippines
May 21, 1945
Dear Warren,

Your May 8 letter came through in eleven days and I don't believe I answered number 98. If we would only get some fresh meat in addition to this good mail service I should know that this is really a rear area.

As I stand with this point system I'll be eligible for discharge in a year if we make two more beachheads. Whatever way you look at it, it aint' good.

Our colonel is a genius by the name of O'Keefe. This outfit....

(Censored by cutting off page.)

Incidentally, I don't care for this barefooted, Technicolor stuff.

Three sergeants in the outfit received direct commissions the other day. I think that method is better than this ninety-day wonder business.

Every Sunday night we have discussions (E.M. only) on such

things as "Bretton Wood", post war economy and so forth. The amazing thing is that twenty-five to forty of this outfit attend. Our speakers are men of this company – usually the Phi Betas, M.A.s and that type.

Still grinding away with the ditcher. I'll have more pictures in a month or two.

Peter

Philippines
June 4, 1945
Dear Warren,

We are now driving on the right hand side of the road again. It will probably change in a few months to the left. Very confusing.

I must be getting behind in my mail. I have number 100, 2 and 4 in front of me. They ranged from 9-14 days. I believe one and three were clippings. Incidentally, the Manter clipping service is widely used.

(This part of letter cut out by censor.)

You are quite correct in number 100 letter about those planes. The Navy also dished it out. I hope the censor does not try to attach any significance to that number.

Peter

Philippines
June 11, 1945
Dear Warren,
There is only time for a quick note. Your letter number 5 came yesterday. There seems to be a number missing.

Everything is much the same here. Hot with rain every afternoon. Oh, yes, your "Adventure" magazine arrived. I wish I had more reading material. On hand I have a Russian novel and a sprightly little tome entitled "The Flowering of New England."

My prediction that I made in the last few letters have gone astray I see. All for now. Some of the boys are going home! The army moved surprisingly fast on the point system.

Sincerely yours,
Peter

The Japanese had been building a concrete strip at Puerto Princessa for over two years with 150 American prisoners of war, mostly survivors of the Bataan death march. Most of the work was by hand with picks, shovels and sledge hammers to break rocks. There was one American concrete mixer and one American crawler tractor, a TD-18.

By December 1944 U.S. B-24 bombers had cratered the 2,200 meters long and 210 meters wide strip so that it was useless although every day the prisoners were sent out to fill the craters.

On December 14, 1944 the prisoners were brought back to camp supposedly for lunch. Air raid warnings sounded and the Japanese soldiers with fixed bayonets ordered the prisoners into their air-raid shelters, slits four feet deep and covered with logs. Then the Japanese poured aviation fuel into the air-raid shelters and set them on fire. Supposedly there were five survivors who escaped into the Sulu Sea and swam to an island where the Filipinos hid them. One survivor wrote a detailed account of this massacre.

Placing the Puerto Princessa strip into operation was a high priority job for the 1897th battalion and we screwed up which must have brought the colonel a reprimand. First the bulldozers were set to filling the water filled craters with the surrounding soil. This was a mistake because the craters were then filled with mud. Then it was necessary excavate the mud from the craters and fill them with sand, rock and coral. The picture shows a hydraulically operated Cat D-8 bulldozer filling

A Caterpillar D-8, the Largest Bulldozer at That Time

craters with rock and gravel. With only two drag-lines for excavation much excavation was done by hand. This was much slower than filling in the craters with bulldozers.

Another error that delayed completion of the air-strip was burning down the asphalt plant. Diesel for cutting back the asphalt was in short supply because a freighter of drummed diesel was torpedoed. Someone decided to use aviation gasoline to cut back the asphalt. The asphalt plant operators used the same temperatures for cutting back the asphalt with gasoline as were used for diesel. The gasoline evaporated, the fumes hit the boiler fires and phoosh, there went the asphalt plant.

Palawan Airstrip

Above is a picture of Palawan Airstrip in operation. The Sulu Sea is at the far end. Most of the coral for the sub-grade was scraped from the Sulu Sea at low tide and hauled to the strip.

In a few weeks there were planes landing and I was assigned to work at the local field hospital. Most of the serious patients were survivors of bomber crashes. I had both a motor grader for fixing the hospital streets and drainage ditches and ditching machine for digging sewer lines.

Note that the controls are all mechanical on this Caterpillar grader.

Grading For a Hospital

The bird colonel in charge of the hospital assigned me a major in medical administration as a rod man for laying out my drainage ditches.

The 1897TH constructed the Puerto Princessa Field Hospital in the picture below. Most of the serious cases were burn victims from plane crashes. Enemy activity was limited.

Field Hospital Puerto Princessa

A quarter-master grave identification company was excavating the slit trenches where the American prisoners-of–war had been burned to death. This was the dry season, the ground was hard and the quarter-master company was digging 150 graves by hand. The quarter-master captain gave my captain a bottle of Scotch to have me assigned to him with my ditching machine to dig the graves.

A ditching machine was fifteen tons of grease points and mechanical problems.

I was also involved in the excavation and reburial of the massacre victims. This was not a pleasant job. After a few hours you became accustomed to the odor but upon returning to camp I removed all my clothes and hung them

Barber Greene Model 44C Ditching Machine

on a bush, walked into camp naked, took a shower, put on clean clothes and had dinner. The next morning I reversed the process, walked out to my dirty clothes on the bush, put them on and returned to my grave excavation and victim burial. The dentist had the worst job. The Japanese had confiscated the dog tags of the prisoners so the primary identification of the prisoners was by dental records. The dentist took teeth molds of all the cadavers.

Moving the 15 ton ditching machine to the cemetery for grave digging was a problem. I had the bright idea of digging graves ahead of time and dug 50 extra graves. The commanding general came by and wanted to know what had happened, had there been a breakthrough? When he found out these were just extra graves he ordered them filled in. The quarter-masters were happy though because digging out the loose dirt was much easier than digging the sun baked soil.

Palawan was much different from Leyte. There were mostly Moros there. No laundry girls. It was drier, not so many banana trees. However there were pineapple bushes and the trick was to find a bush before anyone else and let your pineapple ripen without being stolen. In our company area there was a guava tree. Nobody else knew what a guava was so I had them all to myself.

One day some Moros came to our lieutenant with a sack and said they had something for him. They emptied the sack and out rolled three Japanese heads.

I was on Palawan when the news came that FDR had died. Not long after that came "victory in Europe" and we knew the end of the war was in sight.

CHAPTER 7
Okinawa

Landing by LST on Okinawa

We landed on the Motobu peninsula of Okinawa by LST from Puerto Princessa. The exact date I am not sure of because we were not permitted to date our letters. By the time we landed the Marines had secured the northern part of Okinawa but heavy fighting was taking place in the southern area near Naha. The mission of the 1897th was to build an airstrip across the peninsula.

The following is my first letter from Okinawa.

Not in the Philippines
No date allowed.
Dear Warren,

(The "xxxxxxxxx" indicate words cut out by censor)

Much to my surprise your guess turned out to be correct. It is a pain to go into a place xxx xxxx xxxx xxx and I don't think I am going to xxxxxxxx. Anyway, it is good to be out of the xxxxxxx.

It has been a good trip. Fresh meat, real potatoes and ice cream twice. Beyond hitting the steel deck hard a few times when my jungle hammock collapsed, everything has been peaceful.

One thing I can never understand about the army is its penchant for moving at night in the rain. We sat around for three days and then the first night it started raining we loaded up.

What is this about gum in one of my letters? I don't know how it got there. A friend of mine received a highly indignant letter from his girl friend wanting to know why he enclosed a dead grasshopper with his letter. Don't be surprised if a cobra crawls out of one of my envelopes sometime

The censor enjoyed your note but said the comparison between O'Keefe and Pershing was very far fetched. I agree with him. The clippings were very good.
Peter

My first impression of Okinawa was mosquitoes and flies. The flies were so thick that while eating from your mess kit with one

Okinawan Thatched House

hand you used the other hand to brush the flies off your food. At night the mosquitoes were so thick that their impact against your mosquito bar could keep you awake. The reason for the insect problem was soon apparent. Every Okinawan house had an open cistern for sewage and this was the source of fertilizer for farming. Fortunately the medics had a solution. We soon had Piper Cubs flying overhead spraying the countryside with DDT. The results were spectacular. In one day the flies and mosquitoes disappeared. However, the Okinawan civilians panicked. They thought the Americans were spraying poison gas.

The second letter I wrote from Okinawa follows.

(Another date later than the one not given before.)

Censorship is strict as hell here. We are not even allowed to put in the date. This is an island north of the equator. I can't tell you about the scenery except that it is the prettiest place I have been with rolling hills and stone walls. I can't say anything about vegetation or animal life nor the inhabitants (they are Orientals) nor their way of living, occupation, houses or characteristics. I can't tell anything about the climate specifically. (It is not so humid and the sun is not as hot as the last place) nothing about air raids or fighting if there is any. I am working but I can't tell you what on.

At any rate, Peter D. roared ashore on a ditching machine to dig all the latrines and soakage pits for the battalion and foxholes for the company. Pretty good swimming here and some of us are fixing up a sailboat. I am afraid that you will not hear from me very often. I lost one sheet of this letter in which I answered some of your other letters but number 11 came though here, first one.

My "Time" came through as fast or faster with APO 159 as anyone else's does with the correct APO.

Tell Gloria she should get a tan like mine and then she would not have to worry about the sun. I sent a picture of myself without a shirt to my sister and she said I look like a Filipino. Also it would be a good idea to start her off at the U. of KY her freshmen year if she plans to attend there. Every time you transfer from one school to another there is quite a readjustment that has to be made to teaching methods. I know. My grades took quite a slump my first semester at Cal and it is better to have slump your freshman year than later. Wish I could find the other sheet.

PCAU stands for Philippine Civilian something. I made a mistake.

Peter

94

Motobu Peninsula – Airstrip in Background, Ie-Shima in Distance

We were camped under trees beside the strip we were building with the island of Ie Shima in the distance. There was good coral for building the strip but it was planned over a hump that could not be leveled in the time we were given to build the strip. This was not good because a plane landing at one end could not see the other end of the strip. Air control was not up to professional standards and we had a number of serious crashes as a result.

The following is my third letter from Okinawa

Bulldozing The Way From New Guinea To Japan

(The "XXXXXXX" indicates the censor cut out words)

Western Pacific
July 20

Dear Warren,

On hand I have letters 10,12,13,14. I believe number 11 contained your note to the censor. Lt. Gruska got a kick out of it but he thought the comparison of O'Goof with Pershing was pretty far fetched. I agree with him. The mail service here is remarkable; some letters come through in five days. "The New Yorker" arrives by first class mail in two weeks or less. I guess my sense of humor must be too distorted to enjoy that type of writing.

The subject of weather is verboten but there is a mild XXXXX beating down at present. Otherwise the thermometer hangs at 100-105.

I feel very rural here, parked behind a hedgerow and stonewall in the middle of a comote (type of potatoe) patch. Ducks and chickens wander in and out, goats try to eat your shoes under your bunk and so forth.

Foxholes are no worry to me. I whip them out any length and up to eight feet deep with my ditcher in a few minutes. This is a mechanized war, you know.

Remember when I said things were not going so well? I see why now. We have to chip the tops off the hills and dump them in the valleys. There just is not any level ground.

I know the colonel you mean. Back at the last place O'Goof had him in for chow a few times.

Why in the world does Gloria want to go Denver? That is one of the least attractive cities in the West. If she must go to Colorado tell her to go Colorado Springs.

I have the damnedest time trying to exhaust the QM's supply of 11B, Australian made shoes. No matter how many pair I salvage more comes back. They are leather soled with steel hobnails. When you climb up on a piece of equipment you run a 50-50 chance of breaking a leg.

As for reading material practically anything is good but light reading is usually obtainable over here while most of the more serious novels and nonfiction books never get across. At any rate you have been doing fine and I have no complaints. Your postage bill must be terrific. To answer your request for a request: Please send me reading material. I have some junk to send Bennett.

Peter

Shortly after enough of the strip was finished for landings, General Jimmy Doolittle, the hero of the first bombing of Tokyo, flew in. I was on my bulldozer about ten feet away when he descended from his B-25.

This is another thoroughly censored letter from Okinawa.

(Author's note: This is part of a letter that was either destroyed by the censor or lost. It was apparently written on Okinawa in July. I was writing about my cousin Gloria going to the University of Kentucky.)

The physics is necessary if you are going to handle much electrical apparatus, etc. She will learn how to connect one wire to another and maybe even to replace a burned out fuse.

The paper you and my mother send me is adequate. Don't bother sending me another magazine although...on second thought, the "New Yorker" would be welcome for a little light reading (that V-mail came.) It comes first class; *don't* send it airmail. My mother keeps me supplied with pocket books and we get a batch of paper bound books in the company occasionally that are similar to pocket books but put out by Special Service.

I've been running a grader for the Seabees. The Engineers need only to run at half throttle to keep up with them. Quit for lunch at 11:00 and returned at 13:30. Question: is there a war on?

Peter

The next letter discusses my reading material of which Warren Manter was the most faithful provider and the unprecedented arrival of fresh food.

July 31, 1945
Dear Warren,

Your "Comet" and "Mercury" arrived in a little less than two months. Pretty good time. The book you said that you are sending me sounds pretty good. We don't get that type here at all. I am pretty well set of reading material now with "Time", "New Yorker" and "Stars and Stripes" coming regularly. This is the first place we have been able to get the "Stars and Stripes." (Published in Hawaii.)

The millennium has arrived. For a few days we had fresh meat twice a day and fresh eggs for breakfast.

Damned if I know what to write about. I can't tell you anything that I'd like to. I have been cutting ditches on a road job with a tow grader. Tedious job and lots of mud.

You were not so sharp in No.15. At any rate say hello to Inez and Gloria. I'll write Bennett myself. 16 also arrived July 28.

So long,
Peter

With the strip nearing completion we had a little leisure for exploring. Exploring the Okinawan tombs on the hillsides was a favorite

Okinawan Tomb

pastime. The ashes of the dead are kept in the tombs in jars or vases. One man discovered a box filled with thousands of Japanese yen. He considered the yen to be worthless paper and he passed notes out as souvenirs to anyone who wanted them. When the war ended we discovered that Japanese yen could be redeemed at face value. He had given away hundreds of dollars.

I was able to hitchhike a ride on a C-47 to Ie Shima. There I saw the monument marking the place where Ernie Pyle, the noted war correspondent, was killed by a sniper and I also saw the cross marking his grave.

Monument for Ernie Pyle

A Japanese freighter had run aground offshore from our camp. Our guys went out and removed the refrigeration equipment which they mounted on a Japanese trailer we had confiscated on Leyte. Soon we had a refrigeration plant going with ice for our Cokes and cold beer.

*End of Motobu Airstrip with Bay and Freighter
Aground in Background*

The following letter to Bennett gives some good descriptions of the Okinawan countryside.

(Note: "XXXXXXX" indicates cut out by censor)

Ryukus
August 2, 1945

Dear Bennett,
Censorship has relaxed and can tell you a little about this place. The money comes from a rich farmer's cave that a friend of mine uncovered with a bulldozer. It contained about 15,000 yen.

It is very hilly and rocky here with small flat-topped pines growing in the uncultivated areas. There is very little of the land that is not devoted to some kind of crop. Patches of ground of only a few square feet are terraced off on the sides of hills and planted with sweet potatoes or millet. The low land in the valleys that can be irrigated is checker boarded into rice paddies.

101

Around the houses are patches of cucumbers, cabbage, squash and onions and a few banana and papaya trees.

The houses range from one room thatched huts to fair sized pine lumber or concrete houses with tile roofs and hard wood floors. The rooms are connected by sliding panels and tables are only a foot high because you sit upon the floor. From the books strewed round the natives are highly literate. I even found one book on the armor, firepower, etc. of various battleships including those of the United States.

Along the hills and in the sides of cliffs the inhabitants have dug their tombs. The newer ones are rather elaborate concrete affairs with stonewalls and monuments covered with inscriptions. They all have shelves for vases – evidently they put flowers in them. The bones are kept in jars; some of them are made of fancy porcelain.

Because of the heavy XXXXX all the houses are surrounded by a thick hedgerow of trees. They keep out the wind but certainly provide good breeding places for flies and mosquitoes. When we first arrived the mosquitoes kept you awake from buzzing around outside your mosquito bar.

At first the natives bowed to every American they saw but they have gotten over that now. They are kept in compounds but are allowed to go outside to work.

We have nice little breezes here – anything up to a hundred miles an hour. Some day I expect to see my tent take off like a P-38.

Your father writes that you are a farmer now. That involves nothing but dirt and hard work all the time. I have done all that kind of work that I care to. If there is anything you would like to hear about especially, let me know.
Sincerely yours,

Peter

Ryukyus
August 14, 1945

Dear Warren,

As you may have guessed, censorship has relaxed. I sent Bennett a letter describing the scenic beauties of this place Form 26-325a). Did he by any chance forward it to you? At any rate, I have some pictures of this place and I'll tell you a little about it even if you have read Bennett's letter.

The mail has been coming in slow lately. I have letters 17 and 18 on hand. The news sounds pretty good – so good in fact, they gave us a whole day off for the first time we have been overseas. Radio Tokyo is a riddle; at three o'clock this afternoon they were telling about sinking half the American navy and practically wiping out the Russian army; at four o'clock they were surrendering. And you should hear them rave and rant about the atomic bomb. I still don't expect to be home this year.

You said my letter was dated July 9. They must have held it over quite a while. Your book "With Napoleon in Russia" came slightly mildewed but quite legible. Thanks a lot, that type of book is impossible to find over here.

The war must be almost over. I met two Japs on the road the other evening all dressed up in G.I. clothes. They gave me a big grin and "hello, Joe!" They have not started to bum cigarettes yet but some of them give you the V sign. When we first arrived the Japs were scared silly and bowed to all Americans. They must hate our guts though because we have burned down all the houses possible – sanitary reason mostly.

Yesterday they took our M1s away to prevent too violent a celebration of victory. I feel practically naked without it. Next they'll take away my ditcher I suppose. One thing is certain, there will always be plenty of shovels.

I took the pictures myself – except when I was in them. A "Tournapull" moves 15 cu yards of dirt at 15 miles per hour. This seems to be all I have energy for tonight – I go to work at midnight. I'll describe the countryside in my next letter.

Peter

P.S. no more packages. Your car sounds like it is bad shape. You must have cracked the head.

With the air-strip in operation our training for the next operation commenced. There were inspections by high ranking officers and practically all our heavy equipment was replaced. The next operation was going to be a major one and obviously this could only be the invasion of the Japanese main islands. Apparently we were going to be in the first wave and this would be more serious than our previous actions.

Then, wonder of wonders, the atomic bomb was dropped on Hiroshima followed by Nagasaki and the surrender of the Japanese. We celebrate vigorously with machine gun fire into the sky and some nuts even fired their M-1s firing clips into the air. The next night I gave a lecture to the entire battalion on the source of energy for an atomic bomb based on my course on atomic physics at the University of California.

Sunday, August 19, 1945 the Japanese surrender planes landed on Ie Shima.

Japanese Betty Bombers Painted White with Green Crosses

Our entire battalion was out watching them land. Every binocular, transit and level was in use.

These planes were Betty bombers painted white with green crosses. On Ie Shima the Japanese generals transferred to a U.S. Air Corps C-54 that took them to Manila to negotiate the final surrender terms. Some members of our battalion were on Ie Shima and took pictures of the Japanese generals transferring to the C-54.

Japanese Surrender Team Meeting American Officers

Japanese Boarding a C-54 to Fly to Manila

I have not been able to determine the names of any of the American officers who were the first to speak to surrendering Japanese generals at the end of WW-II.

*General Torashiro Kawabe Boarding
C-54 to Fly to Manila*

When General Kawabe landed in Manila he was met by General Willoughby, MacArthur's chief of intelligence. Willoughby asked Kawabe what language he preferred for the negotiations. Kawabe replied that he had spent a number of years in Berlin as military attaché and that he preferred that the negotiations be in German. This was fine with Willoughby because his native language was German. Thus the original negotiations for the Japanese surrender were conducted in German.

With the surrender, censorship was eliminated and a point system established to determine the priority for being returned home. However most of us would have to go to Japan to repair airfields before being eligible for release from the Army.

The following letters were written after censuring was eliminated

Okinawa
August 24, 1945

Dear Warren,

This damn Army can issue more conflicting reports. One day Stimson says that all men in the Pacific area with 85 point have been "combed out" (guys in this outfit with over 100 points yet!) and the next day some brass bat announces that by October 15 all 85 pointers will be combed out. One day they are going to lower the score; the next day they are not. You don't know what to believe.

About the atomic bomb – I know a little about it. I studied atomic physics – Lawrence is a professor at Cal, Nobel Prize in physics – and friends of mine worked on the project and I have even seen some U-235.

Number 20 arrived today and had a couple of letters before that – mostly clippings – but I cannot find them for confirmation. "Seven Pillars of Wisdom" came through in one month to the day. Very unusual

Tokyo Rose has changed her tune lately. When she sees what goes over Japan shortly, she'll change it even more. They are really preparing a show for the Japs.

For some unknown reason this outfit has been awarded the "Meritorious Service Plaque" or something like that for our Philippines job. Maybe we were not as bad as I thought.

It has been raining lately and we have not had much to do. One of the brains had a stroke and decided that since the war is over we should work two nine-hour shifts a day instead of three eight hour ones. I hope they get over that idea quick. The idea of going to work at three o'clock in the morning does not appeal to me.

I had quite a time today. I hope to be able to tell you about it in the near future. I think I'll get a little sleep before I go to work. Give my regards to Inez and Gloria.

Peter

Okinawa
Sept.6, 1945

Dear Warren

This letter shouldn't be censored so I'll give you all the dope. I have on hand letters 19,19 ½, and 21. Somewhere along the line was a bunch of clippings. A large package of magazines and papers came in good condition. The funny papers were all right but I couldn't find a place to sit down in my own tent for the visitors. Far be it from me to look a gift horse in the mouth but I hope you don't mind my observing that in "The Seven Pillars of Wisdom" chapters fifteen and sixteen occur twice in row while chapters seventeen, eighteen, nineteen and twenty are nowhere to be found.

First it was "One down and two to go", then "Two down, one to go" and now it is "Three down and no transportation." By my calculation I'll be home in March. No one with less than 85 points (May 12) or under forty years old has left yet.

The A. T. C. runs this Motubu strip and do they make a mess of things. One night a PBY and a C-46 loaded with troops crashed head on – one landing, the other taking off. They don't have any crash equipment to speak of, half the time it doesn't work and the crews stand around twiddling their thumbs while the men in the planes toast to death.

One of the clippings you sent mentions the C-54s on Kadena strip. The day I hitchhiked to Kadena by C-47 from Ie Shima the C-54s were lined up as far as you could see. The other day two sailors went out the strip to get a ride to the states. Their luck was really good because they caught a C-54 straight to Berkeley, California, stopping only at Guam – 51 hours. That is good hitchhiking.

We are back in the Sixth Army. They are supposed to invade Kyushu. At any rate, we will move by the end of the month.

In case you don't know the places we have been, here they are: Finchhafen, Maffin Bay, Sansapor, San Pablo and Tanauan on Leyte, Palawan, Motobu Peninsula on Okinawa.

All for now,
Peter

CHAPTER 8
Japan

With our new heavy equipment and past experience, the 1897th was well qualified to bring Japanese airfields up to standard for use by U.S. airplanes. In September 1945 a fleet of LCTs was assembled for the transport of heavy equipment and a troop carrier for the balance of the battalion.

This was the troopship that transported the 1897th from Okinawa to Japan except for the heavy equipment and the heavy equipment operators. The operators went by LCT, three pieces of equipment with operators for each LCT.

The engineers were to be preceded by the 98th Infantry Division (the Pineapple Division) so called because of the shape of their division emblem and also because they trained in Hawaii. The 98th Division had never been in combat.

Map 5 – LCT Route from Okinawa to Wakayama

As noted, our heavy equipment platoons left Okinawa in LCTs, three pieces of heavy equipment per LCT. The equipment operator, of course, was berthed in the LCT along with four or five supporting maintenance personnel. There was little extra personnel space on an LCT and I forget if we doubled up on bunks or slept on the deck.

We immediately encountered a raging typhoon so the fleet commander pulled us up on the beach on the sheltered side of one of the Okinawa islands. It turned out this was the lepers' island. No one sneaked ashore to explore.

In the meantime the typhoon blew the troop transport with the balance of the 1897th far south to the Taiwan area. The wind direction then shifted by 180 degrees and the fleet commander decided that with typhoon behind us we could proceed to Japan. The maximum speed of a LCT is 6 knots. Over a twenty-four period we averaged 11 knots. The typhoon sank two destroyers and damaged a cruiser but our little LCTs rode over the monstrous waves. Most of the LCT crew and the engineers became deathly sick. Our two ensign officers could not get out of their bunk so we navigated by following the lights of the LCT ahead and staying clear of the vessels on the port and starboard. The ship's cook could not get out of his bunk but we had an Italian mechanic who could cook pancakes, spaghetti and meat balls. There was plenty of coffee to wash it down.

The fifteen-ton Barber Greene model 44C ditching machine was 12 feet high and certainly the most ungainly piece of equipment in the battalion. We tied down the ditching machine with two and three inch hawsers from all sides. Even then all watched with concern as we rolled and pitched in that rough storm.

We landed on the beach at Wakayama not far from the Japanese Naval facilities at 2:00 AM, September 26, 1945. I was completely concerned with disembarking the ditching machine and locating it out of the way of the more essential bulldozers that were being off loaded. My M-1 was in my tool box wrapped in plastic but it never occurred to me to get it out even though we were the first American troops to land in this part of Japan. I do not remember any of our platoon carrying weapons ashore. There were no officers with us.

Once ashore we made coffee with blowtorches, gasoline in steel helmets or any other source of fire. Soon an old Japanese dressed in an old style kimono appeared on top of a sand dune near us. We waved at him and he turned around and disappeared. Soon the kids began to arrive and they cautiously approached. I used the few words of Japanese I had learned from my guidebook and that helped. We gave them candy from our C-rations, which they looked at cautiously but did not taste. They turned around and presumably went home with their treasures. By afternoon we had a mixed American-Japanese ball game on the beach.

The following is the first letter I wrote from Japan.

Wakayama, Island of Honshu

Japan
Sept. 29. 1945

Dear Warren,

Numbers 22 and 23 are on hand; damned if I know when I received them. Everything is crazier than hell and everybody is having a picnic.

They presented me with a new ditcher and we left Okinawa by L.C.T. We stayed in a bay for one typhoon and were caught in the tail end of another on the way up. The waves rolled completely over these scows. Our skipper didn't get out of his bunk except for chow and we couldn't get any thing to tie down the equipment. What kept it from rolling right through the side of that garbage barge is beyond me.

The muttonheads landed us on the 26th on the beach three miles from Wakayama at two o'clock in the morning! (9/26) Everyone was so cold that they could not put on enough clothes. (I was soaked from pushing the colonel's jeep out of the surf, the stupid bastard). Eventually the sun came up and soon the Japs started swarming around us. They were quite amazed at the equipment and the kids soon discovered that C rations contain candy and the adults discovered that K rations contain cigarettes.

With the help of our Japanese-English books and much yelling and waving of arms, a brisk trade developed. Cigarettes,

115

sugar and news of Uncle Akio in San Francisco were at a premium. The New Guinea natives were the only people I have run into over here without relatives in San Francisco. Before the day was over you could not move a tractor for fear of squashing kids and a baseball game started with both Japs and Americans playing. You figure it out.

The brains disappeared to find out where we were going and why, so we turned the camp over to the Japs and went sightseeing. We were near a suburban village with a trolley line running into Wakayama. I bought a ticket (enclosed) for twenty sen (100 sen in a yen, one yen is 6-2/3 cents) and traveled all over the city. First chance I get, I am going to Osaka.

Peter

Apparently the first page of my second letter was lost because censoring had ceased. This is the second page of my letter to Warren probably written in October 1945. The letter describes the conditions in Wakayama, which was a Japanese Navy armament site for manufacturing large caliber naval guns.

It is hard to realize that the piles of tile and brick were once a manufacturing city of 200,200. The B-29s did a good job of eliminating the industrial areas and missing the residential districts (including the geisha houses.)

The people are cooperating as much as can be expected. The soldiers and older men meticulously avoid us but otherwise you would not realize that a few months ago we were cutting each other's throats. One night when it was raining we even received invitations to sleep in some of the homes.

The homes are better than I had expected with victory gardens around a lot them and a few with lawns and flower gardens. The houses are made of pinewood or stucco with tile roofs. They had quite a housing program around here with all the houses in one block the same type. The floors are of polished wood and covered with mats. You sit upon cushions on the floor.

(You leave your shoes outside.) The tables are only a foot high and these, with perhaps a vase, painted screen, picture or shelf constitutes the furnishing. The rooms are small but connected with sliding panels so that a number of rooms may be made into one.

Some of the boys are really making money. A package of cigarettes sells for twenty yen and the rations are thirty. On the other hand, a shave, haircut and shampoo only cost one yen.

We are temporarily camped now in a huge steel and munitions factory. Some of the fellows from Pittsburg and Detroit say it compares with anything they have seen.

We are living in an old building for the first time in 19 months.

御 楼 嫌 ヨ タ

Peter *(Signed with 5 Sino-Japanese characters)*

Wakayama Street Scene

The above picture shows a typical Wakayama street scene in 1945. Wakayama was the site of a major Japanese factory and machine shop for the manufacture of large caliber naval cannon. Wakayama was a major bombing target for the USAF and the Air Force used small incendiary bombs for the city and high explosive bombs for the naval factories on the shore. Note that within the city concrete buildings remain standing. Many of the high explosive bombs hit offshore on the beaches and in the surf creating deep craters that were not observable on the surface.

Giggling is the greatest expertise of Japanese girls and certainly meeting Americans for the first time was enough to start them giggling.

Giggling Girls in Wakayama

Here we were with no officers, no chow line, no tents but pup tents, no food but field rations and little money. The nearby trolley line was working so we went to town. We boarded the trolley (densha) paying no attention to placing money in the till. No Japanese argued this point. The city of Wakayama was bombed flat, no stores, no beer joints, and no points of scenic interest. Somehow we heard that in Osaka there were beer parlors open. We found the train station and took the next train to Osaka. This was a high-speed interurban line, crowded, and I stood all the way. Some old women stood up to give me a seat. I declined and then helped them place their bundles on the overhead racks. This action aroused what was obviously pleased comment even though I could not understand the words.

In Osaka with the help of street kids and my few words in Japanese we found the beer hall, Kabaret Kabuki. This was a Japanese version of a German beer hall. The floor was tile, covered with sawdust and there were girls in Japanese dress to bring pitchers of beer. There were no chairs. You stood at tile covered tables and drank your beer with soybeans and tiny dried fish as snacks. I know we paid for this but I forget if we used yen or dollars. Presumably we had been issued actual Japanese currency because I do not remember seeing American invasion currency after the war ended.

Kabaret Kabuki, Osaka

When it came time to leave we discovered we had missed the last train to Wakayama. With the help of street kids we found a hotel, Japanese style, where we slept on the floor and used eastern style toilets. There were eight or ten of us and when I signed the register the proprietor told me we were the first Americans ever to stay at his hotel. In the morning we caught the densha back to Wakayama and thought no more about our trip to Osaka.

One month later I was called into the company commander's office to meet a CID (Criminal Investigation Department) representative. The CID was investigating a big black market organization that used the hotel where we stayed as a headquarters. Not only was my name at the head of the list but also I

Small Town, Kaisuki Machi, Near Wakayama

had stayed at the hotel two days before the Americans landed in that part of Japan. The American landing date was considered to be the date the 98th Infantry Division landed and the landing of engineers was not counted. The Company Commander convinced the CID that I was innocent of any black market activity.

Small towns as pictured above were seldom bombed and most survived the war intact.

Wakayama Electric Rail Station

The electric and steam railroad systems survived the American bombing remarkably well. In September of 1945 the systems between Wakayama, Osaka and the other towns I visited appeared to function normally.

In September of 1945 Japanese women wore only traditional Japanese clothes or, if working, "mompai". The "mompai" dress was dictated during the war because it was the cheapest and plainest material and all the workingwomen were dressed alike. The picture on page 118 of the giggling girls shows the girls wearing part of their "mompai" dress. The coat and pants were formless, loose fitting and all black. Japanese women detested "mompai" and welcomed the end of the war as an excuse to throw away their "mompai."

122

Street Scene, Wakayama

To impress the Japanese, the 98th Division was supposed to make a spectacular landing complete with tanks, field artillery, infantry in full field pack and armed to the teeth. The catch was the infantry needed some engineers on the beach ahead of time with bulldozers and graders to fill in the bomb craters and to level out the roads so the infantry would not be bogged down. The landing would be at

Wakayama where no American troops had yet landed. As mentioned earlier Wakayama was

Landing Craft Bringing 98th Division Troops to Wakayama

the location of major facilities for the manufacture of large Japanese naval rifles. Consequently, heavy U.S. bombers had repeatedly bombed the Naval facilities, leaving the surrounding area, beaches and tidal area pitted with bomb craters hidden under water.

At 4:00 AM September 28, 1945, the troop ship with the balance of the 1897th and the officers arrived as did the 98th Division in landing craft. The 98th Division made the mistake of staging their landing on the beach next to the Japanese naval gun factory. A jeep load of heavily armed soldiers would head for shore and then suddenly disappear. Soon heads would start popping to the surface. We went out on bulldozers and pulled out equipment and

124

rescued soldiers. When the 98th Division finally landed and formed up they marched in formation to Wakayama to give the natives a show although many of the American soldiers were dripping wet. We boarded trolley cars to Wakayama and wildly cheered the Oahu Commandos as we rode by. The infantry was not too pleased.

Barracks at Itami

From Wakayama the 1897th was moved to Itami near Osaka to place the Osaka airport in operation with American aircraft. We were moved to Japanese factory barracks surrounded by a wooden fence. The rooms were small, three to a room, but better than a tent. We even had two old women to clean up for us.

The following is my first letter from Osaka (Itami)

Osaka, Japan
Oct. 26, 1945

Dear Warren,

We have been working the usual seven days a week and I have been fighting a Jap cold, consequently I did not realize that I have not answered 24, 25, 26, 27 or 28.

Your statement about the "Meritorious Service Plaque" is a very exact analysis. By November they will be sending home the fellows from this outfit with over eighty points and I have hopes of getting home by the first of the year. Being eligible for discharge and actually going up the gangplank are two different things.

Upon the ground that things might suddenly change tomorrow, I cautiously state this outfit is having a wonderful time, comparatively speaking. We have moved to Itami airstrip, into Jap air corps barracks. Fresh meat (sheep) and butter have been appearing every day for a week and everyone has a case of Jap beer under his bed. It is only a fifteen-minute ride to Osaka by trolley. I hope I stay here until I ship back.

Things are still screwy. On one side of an apron American crews work on P-51s (the Jap flags painted on the fuselage diplomatically scratched out) while on the other side, Jap ground crews work on Tony Fighters (the stars for American planes diplomatically scratched out.) In the Philippines guards kept civilians without passes out of the area but here Japs wander in and out of the barracks at will. It seems strange talking to some of these pilots who fought in NG, Leyte, Okinawa and so forth on the other side. Incidentally on the two fields where I have been there are at least 150 first line Jap fighters and bombers. If these fields are typical they held a lot of planes in reserve.

My cigarette rations of a pack a day amount to $2.00 a day in actual money. Not bad.

126

A New Yorker should feel at home in Osaka. The subways make New York subways seem about as crowded as Western Texas. I am glad my head travels well up in the fresh air.

The handkerchief is for Inez. It is not very good but I had to buy something. I hope to get a hold of some made out of really high grade silk.

Peter

The Osaka Rail Station Survived Well

It was here that I met a Japanese interpreter, a former lieutenant in the Japanese army, who taught me much about Japan and the Japanese people. Mr. Akiyama was married with a eight year old daughter, Yoshiko. Mrs Akiyama comes from a prominent family, her father was a colonel in the Japanese army. They took me on tours of Kyoto and Nara and other historic sites. At times I stayed in the Akiyama home and was treated to sukiyaki and other Japanese dishes. I always brought along canned chicken or other canned meats and their favorite, American sugar.

The following letter is to Warren's wife, Inez.

Itami, Japan
Nov. 27, 1945

Dear Inez,

There is not a hope of getting home before Christmas. No ships, they say. There certainly was not any shortage of shipping when they moved us into Japan or any other place for that matter. Seventy-one points is the lowest score of anyone shipped out from this outfit.

The weather is getting colder all the time with frost in the mornings. We have a stove in our room but have quite a time keeping it supplied with wood. I hope that I leave before the snow falls.

We have very pleasant quarters here, three men to a room – better than the barracks in the States.

A week or so ago I went to Kyoto for a visit. This city has never been bombed which alone makes it worth seeing. There is a hill there that is covered with temples most of which are a thousand years old. They are made of wood and have never been reconstructed. There are teahouses there that have been in use for almost 500 years. I'll send you a some picture cards, which will be a better explanation than I can give you.

This afternoon I spent shopping – silk handkerchiefs and scarves seemed to be about the best thing to buy. Kyoto has some good department stores but even they have limited supplies and are high priced.

In one of the stores I was talking to the girl interpreter and discover that she was born in the same town I was – Venice, California.

Friday a Japanese family took me on picnic to Nara, one of the oldest cites in Japan. This city contains the oldest wooden buildings in the world – they were constructed 1200 years ago and are the same today as then. The gateway building contains wooden statues fifty feet high and the main temple contains the largest Buddha in the world – a bronze figure fifty-three feet high with fingers four and a half feet long. The Buddha is flanked by four golden Buddhas about thirty feet high.

We ate lunch in the park upon the side of a hill. Tame deer gather around us to beg food. Mrs. Akiyama had brought along a dish of cold rice with mushrooms, welsh carrot, Korean carrot (more of a radish) onions and sprinkled with vinegar, sweet potatoes, tea and tangerines.

I brought bread and jam, a can of salmon and few chocolate bars. It is pretty nice to visit these places with a person who can tell you all about them.

The Akiyamas have a little daughter eight years old by the name of Yoshiko. Because I frequently bump my head in their house, when we are walking Yoshiko often worries that I am going to get my head tangled in the telephone wires or branches of a tree. Mr. Akiyama was in the exporting-importing business and speaks fair English. Mrs. Akiyama is the daughter of a wealthy Kyushu businessman – she went to school with ex-prime minister Kuiso's daughter. I have learned a great deal about the "better" class of Japanese from them.

It is getting late,
Sincerely yours,
Peter

The following is a picture of a shrine I visited in Kyoto.

Shrine in Kyoto

Following is the last letter I wrote in the Army

Itami, Japan
Nov. 27, 1945

Dear Warren,

My writing becomes worse as time goes on. One thing I should like to enlighten you on. The Engineers are never given a chance to sit down and enjoy these sport and educational programs that you may have read about. At first we only worked seven days a week, one shift a day but since the war is over we had to have a half an hour of calisthenics in the morning before breakfast. Can you guess who gives the calisthenics? – The s.o.b.'s. However, work has not progressed fast enough and we are now on two eight-hour shifts a day.

As you guessed, we are lengthening the strip here and making more taxiways. There is a good concrete field with three runways but it is only 5500 feet long. We are making the extensions with asphalt. I have been working on the rock crusher, ditcher, graders and pans. The Japs are quite amazed at this equipment – especially the ditcher. We trained five of them so that they can operate the crusher pretty well. The Japs are not very mechanically minded and when it comes to lifting heavy objects they are pitiful. They are very willing, though, and a lot better workers than the Filipinos.

Don't sneer too much at the cabarets here. The Japs provide the soldiers better entertainment than the city of Richmond did – at a price, of course, but we chisel it back on the black market.

Everything is going smoothly between the GIs and Japs but if some of these guys are not a little more careful about trying to pick up women there may be trouble. There are plenty of dance halls and geisha houses over here for all the occupation forces and the Japs definitely do not like anyone trying to take their wives away from them on trains or in the streets. Some of these guys get a few beers and don't show any sense at all. A number of Japs have remarked to me that they could not understand why Americans drink so much and go out so much with prostitutes. They do not realize at all how their troops behaved away from home.

At present I should say that the attitude toward Americans is a mixture of disdain, envy, indifference and relief that we are not any worse. They also are impressed at how happy Americans are and how much noise we make.

The food situation is worse than it was during the war. Many of the babies are in terrible condition. Skin diseases and eye trouble are prevalent because of the diet deficiencies and lack of soap. Prices are high by any standard. Shoe polish – 15 yen (1 dollar) a jar (10 cent size in the U.S.); cigarettes – 30 yen a pack, oranges – 10 yen apiece. The ordinary day laborer now earns 10-15 yen a day.

The Red Cross recently opened up a recreation hall with sandwiches and coffee in Osaka. The first worthwhile project I have seen the Red Cross accomplish yet. The only other entertainment is movies, dance halls and geisha houses. The worst thing about going out at night is the transportation. The subways and trains are more crowded every day.

The teenage girls are getting movie struck. They dress up in short skirts with silk stockings and lots of lipstick and rouge and go to the railroad station to pick up soldiers to take them to American movies.

Kyoto and Nara are the only cities that have not been bombed. Kobe was 80% eliminated. I have been to both Kyoto and Nara. Kyoto is especially nice. I'll write Inez and you can learn about my travels from her.

Peter

(Note: 33 the last letter.)

The initial task at the Osaka airport was destroying the Japanese aircraft there. There was a shipment of new Betty bombers, just out of the factory. We lined them up, pushed them into a gigantic pile, drenched the pile with gasoline and burned the pile. The planes burned for a week. The strip had to be lengthened and my main job was improving the drainage system around the airport. Japanese kids everyplace wanted to ride on a bulldozer. I would make them line up and take a turn, one at a time. They would bring me presents like fresh onions.

Finally our point system added up and we were eligible to return to the States. We were moved to near Tokyo, the battalion was disbanded and we settled down to wait for shipping space. Before Christmas 1945 I was on a troop transport headed for Seattle. On Christmas we were off the Aleutians in a severe storm. Many were seasick and worse, our Christmas turkey was bad and everyone who was not seasick had diarrhea. We landed quietly in Seattle and were placed on a train to Fort Lewis. From Fort Lewis I went by train to Camp Beale, California, to be discharged on January 7th, 1946. I arrived at Oceanside on a Saturday to be met by my mother for the drive home. Sunday I received a job driving a bulldozer for a local construction outfit and went to work on a Caterpillar D-2 on Monday morning.

REFERENCE	DESCRIPTION
A.T.C	Army Transport Command
Ack-ack	Anti-Aircraft. British term we picked up from the Aussies.
B-25	Twin engine, light bomber made by North American. Crew of four.
Betty Bomber	American name for a two engine Japanese bomber.
Bulldozer, Underwater	Diesel bulldozer with intake and exhaust extended and all block openings such as the crankcase oil measuring stick sealed. Could operate in up to 8 feet of water.
C-46	Curtis two engine transport plane
C-47	Twin engine transport plane. In civilian life it was known as a DC-3.
C-54	Four engine military transport plane.
C-Ration	Canned ration containing mixtures of meat, starch and vegetables.

Cat	Refers to a Caterpillar tractor.
D-7	Four cylinder, diesel engine bulldozer. Second heaviest made by Caterpillar.
D-8	Six cylinder, diesel engine bulldozer. Largest tractor made by Caterpillar at that time.
Daisy Cutter	Japanese anti-personnel bomb weighing one or two pounds. Hundreds were dumped from a bomber at one time.
DUKW (Duck)	6x6, 2-1/2 ton amphibious truck.
Enfield Rifle	The Enfield rifle was the standard infantry weapon of the British Army.
Flak	Falling fragments of shells exploding overhead. Primary reason we wore steel helmets.
Grease Gun	.45 caliber, short barrel, compact, magazine fed, sub-machine gun.

LCT	Landing Craft Tank, displacement 286 tons, load 150 tons, see Appendix B for details.
LCVT	Landing Craft Vehicle Troop
LST	Landing Ship Tank for amphibious operations , 4000 to 5000 ton landing ship (there were a number of versions), for tanks, heavy equipment and personnel. Two decks. See Appendix B for details.
K-Ration	Boxed ration containing cigarettes, crackers and meat.
M-1 Carbine	Light weight weapon for officers and non-coms, 30 caliber, gas operated, rotating bolt, 15 or 30 round detachable box magazine, semi-automatic.
M-1 Rifle	Basic WW-II infantry weapon. Clip fed, 8 shot, 30 caliber, gas operated, semi-automatic rifle
P-38	Twin engine Lockheed fighter plane. With detachable gas tanks this was a good plane for the long distances of the Pacific.

PBY | Two engine Consolidated flying boat used by the Navy for long distance patrols. One version was amphibious.

TD-18 | Large diesel engine crawler type tractor manufactured by International Harvester.

Tommy Gun | Thompson Sub-machine Gun. Basic sub-machine gun of the U.S. Army at that time. 45 caliber, medium barrel, magazine fed, can be switched from fully automatic to semi-automatic.

Tuba | A naturally fermented alcoholic beverage from the bud at the top of a coconut palm tree

Tournapull | Primary dirt mover manufactured by Le Tourneau company. A two wheeled rubber tired diesel tractor pulled a two wheel rubber tired carryall operated by cable . See Appendix B.

Zero | Single engine Japanese fighter plane.

Tournapull

Military Tournapull & Carryall Scraper

A two wheeled Tournapull Super C tractor powered by a Cummings diesel engine pulling a two wheeled LP Carryall scraper, cable operated from the tractor. This size carryall held 15 cubic yards that the tractor could pull at 15 miles per hour. There were similar carryalls but four wheeled for the D-8 and D-7 Caterpillar tractors and they carried 12 and 10 cubic yards.

The Tournapull required a push tractor to load the carryall. The tractor was steered with steering clutches and individual brakes on each wheel. Only the most skillful and best coordinated operators were allowed to operate this equipment. While pulling the carryall, pulling the right clutch turned the tractor to the right but if you were slowing down or going down hill pulling the right clutch turned the tractor to the left. An operator error could be catastrophic with 35 tons of wet sand in the carryall behind you moving 15 miles per hour.

LST – Landing Ship Tank

LST Photo from the Bow

This bow picture of an LST illustrates how an LST went into action. This 5000 ton shallow draft vessel would drive up onto a beach with a stern anchor set out to drag the ship back into deep water. The Engineers customarily had an underwater bulldozer just inside the front doors so it would be the first vehicle off. The bulldozer would go ashore and bulldoze a ramp up to the front doors so that the following vehicles would not have a problem with deep water or shell or bomb craters

There are two decks to an LST. All vehicles entered through the front doors but there was an interior ramp leading to the top deck where trucks, jeeps and other light weight vehicles were carried. Heavy vehicles such as tanks, bulldozers and construction equipment were carried on the bottom deck. The LST crew had bunks but passengers such as GIs had to find a bare piece of deck to sleep on or hang up a jungle hammock.

Notice above in the bow the twin Bofors 40mm antiaircraft guns. These were the principle armament of an LST. They also carried 20 mm cannon for low flying planes. LSTs were thin walled and armor piercing machine gun fire and any kind of higher caliber fire would penetrate.

DUKW – Amphibious Truck

DUKW – 6x6 Amphibious Truck

The **DUKW** (popularly pronounced *"duck"*) is a six-wheel-drive amphibious truck that was designed by General Motors Corporation during World War II for transporting goods and troops over land and water and for use approaching and crossing beaches in amphibious attacks.

Caterpillar D7 Track Tractor

Cat D7 Tractor

The Caterpillar D7 tractor shown here as used in WW-II weighed 15-1/2 tons fitted with Le Tourneau cable controls and a bulldozer blade. The cable controls were necessary instead of hydraulic controls because it was frequently necessary to remove the blade and attach the tractor to another cable operated piece of equipment such as a carryall scraper. Also the operators like the cable rig clearing jungle because the headache bar offered some protection from falling trees.

The D7 was powered with a four cylinder Caterpillar diesel engine producing 92 horse power at 1,050 rpm. The transmission was 5-speed with a 2-speed transfer case so that there were 10 speeds total.

The nightmare was the two cylinder gasoline starting engine on the left side of the diesel engine. This engine was hand cranked from either the top, the front or the side. The starting engine was started with the diesel transmission in neutral, the diesel compression control pulled out, the governor control turned off (no throttle, the diesel was governor controlled) and the starting engine clutch and gear to the diesel engine disconnected. Cranking the starting engine would start it providing there was gasoline in the starting engine tank, rust was not blocking the gasoline fuel line, tropical humidity had not shorted out the ignition system and the two spark plugs did not need cleaning.

Once the starting engine was running you waited for it to warm up because the starting engine exhaust preheated the diesel engine intake air. When the starting engine was running smoothly you then pushed in the gear to the diesel engine and let out the starting engine clutch. Because the diesel engine compression had been released the starting engine could turn the diesel engine easily. When the diesel engine was turning rapidly you then pushed in the compression control. If the starting engine did not stall, the diesel engine was now turning over under full compression but with no fuel. In cold weather it was then necessary to wait for the diesel engine to warm up but in the tropics you could immediately turn on the governor control and the diesel engine would roar into action and then slow down as the governor took over. When the diesel engine was running faster than the starting engine, the starting engine would automatically kick out. Then you shut off the starting engine, turned of the valve at the gasoline tank and drained the gasoline line in hope that this would prevent line plugging the next time you wanted to use it.

We did not shut down our Caterpillar diesel engines when we stopped for lunch.

LCT- Landing Craft Tank

The LCT had a number of versions but this version was 114 feet long, 32 feet wide, displaced 286 short tons and could carry 150 short tons. The maximum speed was 7 knots and its range was 700 miles. Armament varied but generally only 20 mm antiaircraft and 50 caliber machine guns were carried.

Acknowledgements

Wally McPhee for his meticulous proofing and corrections.

Peter Mele for his many hours formatting this book and preparing it for publication

Nick and Mary Mele for encouraging me to compile my letters, pictures and notes into a book about Army life in New Guinea and the South Pacific.